CHEON OF THE NEVER NEVER

A life member of the Chinese Historical Society and the Cairns and District Chinese Association Inc., and founding member and president of Chinese Heritage in Northern Australia Inc., Kevin Wong Hoy has made a significant contribution to Chinese Australian history. Descending from cane farmer and community leader Willie Ming and Gulf of Carpentaria bakery and butcher shop owner Yet Hoy, he has always had an interest in Northern Australian history and heritage. He has written and edited books and journals, has been interviewed for radio programmes, and was a consultant for a Chinese archaeological site.

CHEON OF THE NEVER NEVER

KEVIN WONG HOY

ARCADIA

First published 2012, reprinted 2016, Arcadia, the general books' imprint of
Australian Scholarly Publishing Pty Ltd
7 Lt Lothian St Nth, North Melbourne, Vic 3051 TEL: 03 9329 6963 FAX: 03 9329 5452
EMAIL: aspic@ozemail.com.au WEB: scholarly.info

ISBN 978-1-921875-86-1

Design and typesetting Sarah Anderson
The main chapters of this book are typeset in Minion Pro 10.5pt

For Chloe Rose

CONTENTS

Preface vii

Introduction 1

1 The 'Tiger' Man and the 'Whitest' Man Together 16

2 Cheon at Bradshaw's Run, Victoria River 32

3 Cheon at Carlton Hill Station with the Alfred Martin Family 45

4 The Gilruth Regime, Cheon and His Cooking Rivals 52

5 Cheon and Dr Leighton-Jones, Chief Medical Officer for the Northern Territory 67

6 Cheon Cooks for One of Darwin's Most Commercially Powerful Men 72

7 The Real Cheon Farewells Australia and Returns Home 82

Epilogue 90

Notes 95

Bibliography 104

Acknowledgements 108

PREFACE

In all probability, Cheon, the cook, would not have been introduced to a reading public more than a hundred years ago had the London publishing house of Hutchinson & Co. not agreed – with some reservation about the vagueness of the title – to publish Mrs Aeneas Gunn's manuscript, which appeared in 1908 as *We of the Never Never*. The manuscript had been knocked back by several publishers before it arrived at Hutchinson's. Had the story not been written or published, a Chinese Australian of significance would have received almost no public exposure and might well have slid from the grasp of Australian history altogether.

Deepening Chinese Australian historical research can be a demanding responsibility for its devotees, particularly if the researcher attempts to look beyond petty racial opinion or political agenda. In fact, the scholar of Chinese Australia needs not infrequently to explore archival repositories without map or compass, to read between the lines in English and sometimes in Cantonese, and to connect up random annotations in order to keep a particular quarry in sight. The hunt in this endeavour was assisted immeasurably by the text of *We of the Never Never* and the personal notes composed by Jeannie Gunn, both of which can be used much as a guidebook to the highlights of Cheon's history.

We of the Never Never is, essentially, an early twentieth-century memoir about the life of a cattle station; the events described in it occur over a thirteen-month period during 1902–03. The outline of the story tantalised with the promise of travel, adventure, humour, pathos and the unexpected from an exotic and little known location: the Northern Territory of Australia. Despite the substantial shipping to and from Port Darwin harbour since European settlement in 1869, and the north–south path of the Overland Telegraph Line which connected Australia by cable to the rest of the world from 1872, the notion of the North's remoteness and isolation long persisted in the public imagination – and possibly still does.

We of the Never Never celebrated white masculinity and superiority. On the one hand, this could take the form of bush chivalry, but on the other it could appear as a form of outback male chauvinism. Notwithstanding the latter, it seemed that a petite woman with openness, friendliness and self-deprecating humour – the new station manager's Melbourne-born wife – might still come to occupy a significant role and command no little respect in such a world, as might a male Chinese cook of exceptional capabilities and a big personality.

As the wife of Aeneas Gunn, the incoming manager of Elsey cattle station, Jeannie Gunn had the good fortune of being married to a man who had already gained the acquaintance and respect of the European locals during his earlier, extended periods spent in the north. From the equanimity and good humour of the new boss towards almost all events that come his way, a reader might take from *We of the Never Never* a sense of general positivity. An assortment of lively characters emerge as the memoir unfolds – stockmen, townsfolk, fun-loving Aboriginal children, Chinese cooks, Aboriginal men and women of the station, transplanted Britons and Scots and Irishmen, and other travellers. Figuring no less memorably in the book are the station's work-horses and homestead dogs, the seasonal Dry and the Wet, the Overland Telegraph and, indeed, the outback itself. It was the interaction among all these and the straightforwardness of Jeannie Gunn's writing that gave spark to the story. When death cast its long shadow over Elsey Station, the construction of the book's final chapter and the philosophical stance taken by the author left little room for lingering remorse.

Although Cheon's considerable celebrity had been promoted through Jeannie Gunn's written account, Cheon himself showed little serious interest in exploiting this fame but was nonetheless happy to talk about his former mistress if an occasion arose. Had a contemporary entrepreneur offered to manage his celebrity, perhaps Cheon's Australian story might have been very different. Let us not forget that Cheon had earned a certain reputation by his own efforts also: he had found local recognition among Territorians as both a regional personality and a chef. Yet it was surely Jeannie Gunn's account of his attributes, mannerisms and activities that launched him before an audience of admirers (and not just the English-speakers) well beyond the perimeters of Australia's Top End.

Even so, Cheon's depiction as a cheerful, energetic, opinionated and likeable character who contributed much to the humour in the book did not ensure that diligent research would lead us to his real-life identity, as it did for several of the other characters, specifically the white settlers. Uncertainty about Cheon's true Chinese name may have arisen because of the use of various different transliterated English language versions of it. However, while dissertations about Cheon have not advanced our understanding of him to any major extent, there was nonetheless an undeniable level of public interest in him and what became of him. Had research into Cheon's identity occurred soon after the publication of *We of the Never Never*, it could have done much to record details about him and his origins.

Neither Cheon's involvement in the Northern Territory nor his contact with Jeannie Gunn concluded when the account contained in *We of the Never Never* drew to a close in 1903. Cheon continued cooking in the Territory for a further fifteen years and maintained correspondence with his former mistress for a similar period. The greater part of his post-*Never Never* history awaits the telling.

A desire to discover Cheon's real Chinese name and as much as possible about his real life in Australia has inspired my research. *Cheon of the Never Never* is the result of that effort.

Kevin Wong Hoy
North Melbourne
November 2012

INTRODUCTION

From the outset, I have a confession concerning *We of the Never Never*, ostensibly one of Australia's literary classics: knowing of its existence and reputation long proved an insufficient inducement for me actually to read it. Was it the dread of revisiting yet again the stereotyped Chinese characters of much early Australian literature that kept me and the *Never Never* apart? Regardless of many such detrimental experiences, a pre-loved copy of the book had still found a space on one of my bookshelves. Plainly, this reluctance towards my reading of the book had been shaped by prejudice, and prejudice, in wherever form it comes, should never be allowed to go uncontested. So, on principle, I challenged myself at the very least to sample the narrative of *We of the Never Never*, mustering as much open-mindedness and equanimity as possible.

Unbeknown to me at the time, an additional incentive to get on with this self-challenge would come from a couple of different sources. A desire to locate qualitative descriptions of Chinese cooking in late nineteenth- and early twentieth-century Australia – for an historical talk that I had agreed to deliver – made it necessary for me to search for relevant material. Preliminary research indicated that reading Jeannie Gunn's book might supply details of interest. Around the same time, Baz Luhrmann's splendid film *Australia* (2008) started screening in Australian cinemas. Set somewhere in our remote Top End, the film offered encouragement of a more subtle kind. As part of an audience, intermittently lit by flashes reflected from the cinema screen – the latter sometimes filled by the larger-than-life images of our Australian film stars Hugh Jackman and

Nicole Kidman, and by Hong Kong stunt actor Wah Yuen (cast as the Chinese station cook) – I came to accept that the time had come to get better acquainted with *We of the Never Never*.

Once having opened my mind to Jeannie Gunn's book, delight and amazement at its contents soon followed. By sharing her recollection of life on the Elsey cattle station, Gunn launched publicly a variety of strongly drawn characters, not the least among them being the robust, lively personality known as Cheon, the station cook and gardener. Surprising differences emerged between this character and what was usually found in contemporaneous Australian literature. In addition to the complex nature of Cheon's character, there was the unexpected predominance of his role – particularly when one considers that the *Never Never* manuscript came into existence during the giddy ascendency of the White Australia Policy. Having become too immured by the sort of Australian writing that cast Chinese as the undifferentiated, 'alien' other or as a major danger to national security and racial sanctity, I was suitably chastened to realise that accumulating a certain amount of dust on my own bookshelf had been an early twentieth-century literary work featuring a 'breakout' representation of a Chinese Australian historical figure.

Most likely, more than a million copies (either abridged or unabridged) have been purchased since the book was first published. *We of the Never Never* accrued a vast readership. Some copies, however, due to the vagaries of human nature, may have been placed unread, even unopened, on a bookshelf, but for the majority who read the book, Cheon found a position among the best known characters in Australian literature. Appropriate to the character's pivotal role, Cheon's name appeared many more times in the account than that of almost every other character. And yet, I wondered, did the significance of the Chinese cook's centrality in the narrative register with readers?

The digitisation of Australian newspapers has been a boon, making it easy and quick to identify numbers of articles mentioning *We of the Never Never*. Four such articles that acknowledge Cheon's presence have been selected for their appreciation of him – one published by South Australia's *The Advertiser* (1909); another by the *Northern Territory Times and Gazette* (1919) supposedly reprinted from the Sydney *Sun*; a third by the *Northern Standard* (1932) of the Northern Territory; and lastly, a

Cheon, shortly before he sailed from Darwin. Photograph: WJ Barnes

rapturous piece by a 'special contributor', published by *The Sydney Morning Herald* (1926).

While many a perfunctory booklist published in early twentieth-century newspapers advertised the availability of *We of the Never Never* – at times misleadingly, under the banner of 'New Fiction'[1] – the Adelaide *Advertiser* also printed an extensive article about the book's author, as well as Cheon and the other characters in the story. In this article, which appeared some eight weeks after the first consignment of the book had reached Melbourne, *The Advertiser* claimed brightly of these characters that 'they one and all represent human nature at its best', as it endeavoured to provide a comprehensive appraisal of the work. As the reviewer appeared to have had so favourable a reaction to the Never Never characters, the article speculated that 'one would almost think that people become more civilised the further they are removed from civilisation'. Of particular importance, the article stated explicitly that while the book was perceived by some as a novel, 'it is rather a collection of reminiscences' – or in other words, a non-fiction work. As for Cheon, he was described with the following words:

> [A]nd last, but not least, the irrepressible Cheon, the Chinese cook and gardener, where could a more delightful company be found? ... The picture Mrs Gunn gives of the famous Christmas dinner, at which Cheon excelled himself in the culinary art might also have come from the pen of Dickens. Four dozen eggs in a pudding necessitates an all-night boiling, but in his anxiety to monopolise the honors Cheon would allow no one to share the long watch with him.[2]

A decade later, a young woman traveller's commentary about her visit to Darwin included reference to the surviving, flesh-and-blood Territory residents behind the *Never Never* story. However, rather than keeping the characters frozen in time, she updated public perceptions by reminding us that Cheon had become an elderly man since Aeneas Gunn was the manager of Elsey Station. Regardless, it seemed that 'irrepressibility' would forever be associated with Cheon's name.

> The fascination of knowing someone who has been 'put in a book' never loses its hold, and some of the characters made public property by Mrs Gunn, are still living in the Territory, Cheon, irrepressible Chinese cook, is getting pretty old, but the Sanguine Scot still chuckles over the adventure with the horses.[3]

Jeannie Gunn, too – from a newspaper interview another decade and a half later on – added to the transformation of Cheon's public image from that of energetic station cook to senior member of his own family group. Although it has been difficult to differentiate Gunn's personal expression from that of the journalist, this extract, whether intentionally or not, alluded to two conservative Chinese cultural concepts with relevance for interacting with the elderly: one was the traditional Chinese philosophy that directed the young to respect the elderly, such as Cheon now was; the other was the social etiquette of addressing those with respected status. As Cheon became a venerated elder, it was not so much the size of the Chinese characters in his name that mattered but the fact that the term 'Ah' had become inappropriate for him, since it is usually used in a familiar way that is more applicable for juniors or subordinates.

> As Cheon's relatives died, and he became a big man in China, with a new and important signature, which sent to Mrs Gunn each year looks strange next to the little scrawl which represented the signature of Ah Cheon, the cook.
>
> When Mrs Gunn last heard from Ah Cheon he was getting old and feeble.[4]

The fourth item attested that Cheon was a 'gentleman, high class, not a coolie'. This claim holds a certain validity, especially when one looks beyond his lack of fluency in English and imagines him expressing his

Aeneas J Gunn –
the 'whitest' man, reproduced from Alfred Searcy, *In Northern Seas* (1905).

thoughts or ideas unimpeded by imperfect vocabulary and grammar. Importantly, this article, written by A.L. Williams, included Cheon along with several of the other major 'real' characters, describing them all as exemplars of our Australian way of life. Although not undeserved, this was appreciably greater recognition of Cheon than was generally paid to him.

> Few Australians will admit they do not know the Fizzer, the 'Little'un', the Maluka, the three Macs and Cheon, immortal figures in the gallery of Australian literature.

> We all have our favourite characters in fiction, but we reserve a special niche in our affection for the 'real' characters in Mrs Aeneas Gunn's *We of the Never Never.* Whether Australian born, or Australian by adoption, we know them in the bone of our bone, and flesh of our flesh, who by the chronicling of their lives, thoughts, and ideas, have drawn the sympathy of the world to those who, sacrificing the amenity of the cities, have lived their lives in the wayback.[5]

Basically, newspaper articles about *We of the Never Never* divide into two types: those that make reference to Cheon and those that do not. Already discussed are the articles containing a reasonable awareness of Cheon, although not necessarily of his significance. On the other side are those articles that conscientiously avoid mentioning him and any other non-white character. These two newspaper pieces discussed below, supposedly written as book reviews, have, in addition, each been appropriated by the commentator to serve another function.

An article on *We of the Never Never* published in early 1909 by *The Sydney Morning Herald* under the heading 'An Australian Woman's Book' was not credited to any particular reporter, but, by the tone and trajectory of the piece, it may have been the work of a female journalist. The breadth and scope of the *Herald* doubtless permitted the newspaper to select headings that ran the risk of division among its readership. The strong whiff of the feminine world suggested by the heading had the potential to alienate a certain class of male reader. When the article was published, women's suffrage in Australia had not long been achieved, with the state of Victoria being the last jurisdiction to grant its women the vote, in 1908. Even so, some Australian men might still be heard muttering about these changes.

One could imagine the *Herald* journalist settling with some relish to her task of reviewing the new book, for it afforded opportunity to spruik the superior, perceptive abilities of its author. Opening with a statement in praise for what a female writer can do, the article applauded the positivity of Jeannie Gunn's literary style.

> It has remained for a woman to write the truth about Australia, and to paint in natural, normal colours the lives of the people 'out back'. In her book, *We of the Never Never*, Mrs Aeneas Gunn gets right away from the conventional idea – arisen no one knows how – that the Australian bush is full of morbid, sordid experiences,

> and gloom and melancholy. There is none of the weird expectancy of the bush, in her story; none of the animal degeneracy which characterises too many of our writers' works. She tells in easy, pleasant language of a year spent out in the Great Gulf country, right out in the Never-never, and it is a year which any woman might envy her, so full was it of incident, occupation, and amusement.[6]

While celebrating the superiority of a female writer in the largely male domain of depicting the Australian outback, having to discuss several of the conventional hallmarks of womanhood could not be escaped. In fact, some sectors of the female readership of the *Herald* would have empathised with the wifely duties described – a wife supporting her husband's work, selecting suitable and practical clothing for herself, making do in the interim, and creating a home for herself and her spouse. Focusing on the determination of the main female character and the book's author rolled into one, the article highlighted her agency in establishing a home, even though the timber for the dining room and other sections of the homestead, at a certain stage in the *Never Never* narrative, was still in the form of unfelled trees.

> [B]ut when a woman wants to make a house it takes more than that to stop her; and so the 'little missus', as she is known to the station, has her way, and the dining room and rest of the house are carried from the forest and made into the home she wants. The account of this home-building is one of the most delightful scenes in the book; how the men make journeys backwards and forwards to Katherine – a couple of hundred miles – for the tools and materials they need; how a sawpit is got going in the bush, and the best trees are chosen, felled, and by degrees converted into beams and joists and flooring boards; how the furniture is made up of odds and ends of packing cases; how a fly proof dining-room is erected of mosquito net and unbleached calico, and how at last, with the arrival of the waggons with the books and curtains and blue matting, the hut is finally transfigured into a home. Indeed, it is a description that will appeal to every woman, even if her own home building has never gone further back than the furniture shop and the upholsterer.[7]

As *We of the Never Never* ventured specifically into the vexing question of female–male relations, so too did the article. A number of events described how outback men 'fear' intervention by women. One of these events was Jeannie Gunn's impending arrival and her determination to reach Katherine and subsequently Elsey Station despite the arrival of the big Wet. Another event recounted in the book – but not cited in the article – was her offer actively to assist by riding over to Warloch Ponds to administer to a man sickened with fever. With the issue summarised in the article, we gain a glimpse of the male chivalry and chauvinism of the outback.

> But more interesting even than the things she does are the people she meets. The men on the station, who after opposing her coming in every possible way because they fear a 'goer', completely surrender to her when they find what a little thing she is, and one and all become the firm friends and allies of the 'little missus'. And before you have finished the book you envy her the friendship of those plain bushmen, each one of whom is pictured faithfully and convincingly. Their ways are not city ways, and their manners not ours, but they are men to tho core. 'Bushmen will risk their lives for a woman, pal or otherwise, but will leave her to pick up her own handkerchief. Of course,' that added after an afterthought, 'it's not often they find a pal in a woman', and I add to-day that when they do, that woman is to be envied by her friends.[8]

The article concluded by focusing on the ordinary folk fulfilling their daily duties. With these closing paragraphs, a distinctly romantic tone had crept into the report as a 'Banjo' Paterson ballad, 'Clancy of the Overflow', was seemingly being called to mind while the journalist tapped at her typewriter or drummed her finger-tips as she wrote. The reporter found compelling the comparison between the 'softness' of city living and the seemingly unsullied life in the outback. Yet, completely absent in the entire 'review' was any reference to Cheon, or to other non-white characters. So assiduously had the reporter avoided any mention of Cheon, and of his not inconsequential role, that she was forced to steer clear of making any reference to cooking and the logistics of feeding hungry outback workers, even though these count as critical duties. As a direct consequence, Cheon's Christmas feast – doubtless, one of the great highlights of Jeannie Gunn's time at Elsey Station – was completely passed over.

> The book is filled with the accounts of everyday people doing everyday things. There are the cattle musters, the brumby hunts, and the horse-breaking; there

> are the bullock-punchers, the mailman, the men who look after the telegraph line, and the men from beyond, passing outward or inward. To these men their daily occupations are as natural and matter-of-fact as the rising of the sun, or the boiling of their billy; but to us in the city they seem surrounded with such peril and difficulty that one gasps in wonder as to how they can ever face them. With our post three times a day, our butcher's meat delivered at the door, our every want supplied in half an hour by means of a telephone message, it is hard to believe that the mailman who travels alone on his thousand-mile ride to deliver letters in the very Back of Beyond, and the man who has his letters addressed 'Brown, Esq., in charge of stud bulls going West, via Northern Territory', are fellow-countrymen. But they are, and they think no more of their conditions than we do of walking down Pitt-street. It is all part of their day's work, to be done the best they can. And it is just because these men go on their way simply and naturally, that we in the cities can live in peace and plenty, secure in the knowledge that the great heart of our country is beating steadily and strong.[9]

The Bulletin, too, in early 1909, devoted almost two columns of its 'Red Page' to reviewing *We of the Never Never*. Like the *Sydney Morning Herald* piece, the article in *The Bulletin* was devoid of references to Cheon or to his cooking. If the article had not reminded readers that Mrs Gunn was the acclaimed author of *The Little Black Princess*, it would similarly have cut out all of Indigenous Australia.

Well known for its hostile and belittling opinions of Chinese, *The Bulletin* enjoyed a readership that seemingly chortled or smirked over its plethora of racist commentaries and cartoons. In publishing its literary review of *We of the Never Never*, *The Bulletin* exhorted 'all good Australians' to read it, yet most uncharacteristically refrained from printing any derogatory racial remarks about Chinese or – its other favourite target – Aborigines. What it did was simply to disregard their presence in the book. Failure to mention or acknowledge was not a rare occurrence among sophisticated racists. Not mentioning Chinese or Aborigines stood as a metaphor for their imaginary, ideal Australian landscape peopled solely by whites. Yet to overlook completely one of the *Never Never*'s main characters in the form of Cheon constituted a literary misdemeanour of serious proportions. Still, even with such a major omission, *The Bulletin* did encourage its readers to examine the book's contents. One has to speculate whether they read with objectivity or otherwise.

> *We of the Never Never* ... is a book that is cordially recommended to all good Australians. Not that, it is an exciting yarn, a well constructed story; or a charming romance; it is the simple gracefully recorded account of one year of life of the Territorians – a year spent by the author upon the homestead of 'The Elsey', a great cattle run three hundred miles from a town, somewhere on the track of the overland telegraph. To that station the author, the wife of the new boss, went fresh from the ignorance of the South, and there, by the cordial and, at times, almost unkindly assistance of the staff, she gradually 'learnt things'. But she brought to that exotic life a ready tact, a generous sympathy, a fierce energy, an over-brimming good humour, and a graceful pen.[10]

But subverting its review, *The Bulletin* pursued its principal intention of promoting increased white settlement in the seemingly vast and empty, yet paradisiacal, portion of Australia: the Northern Territory. Could it be that acknowledging the existence of a pivotal protagonist such as Cheon in a work of non-fiction would have meant that *The Bulletin*'s vision of a White Australia had been compromised by a different reality?

> But quite another picture is given of the station. Here is a paradise – ever-flowing streams, a plethora of bird life, good feed for cattle and horses, a fine climate, and as Mrs Gunn has proved, the possibility of a comfortable and rational white-man's life. The run comprised a couple of thousand square miles of scrub and open timbered country, and at the homestead lived a colony of White Men ...
>
> ... and in spite of those hundreds of thousands of square miles of bushland, the people of the Territory are held together in one great brotherhood.
>
> So there is this great empty section of continent waiting, waiting ...[11]

If the abovementioned newspaper pieces proved unconvincing with regard to Cheon's importance, then some other publications offered a variety of introductions to him. From the following assortment of journal articles, book chapters and monographs that discuss *We of the Never Never* or its author, several presented stimulating snippets of information about Cheon, and others not so much.

Geneviève Hauriou, in her thesis 'Un Auteur Australien: Mrs Gunn' (1928), could have been the first to carry out an academic analysis of Jeannie Gunn's work. The novelty for Australian literature is that this dissertation was written in French. In keeping with the text of *We of the Never Never*, this analysis employed a string of adjectives to present Cheon: '*Et Cheou! l'inimitable Cheou, le cuisinier chinois gras, énorme, volubile, important, grotesque, mais au coeur d'or, inlassablement dévoué, et d'un savoir-faire universale*'. In translation, not unexpectedly, Cheon was described as the fat, huge, talkative, devoted Chinese cook with a heart of gold and a good, general expertise. Hauriou added further descriptors: '*important*' and '*grotesque*'. In so doing, ambiguity arises as to her intention. She is perhaps the only commentator to appreciate just how dominant and influential Cheon emerges in the story. However, according to an earlier meaning of the word, '*important*' can also be interpreted as 'pretentious'. In attributing '*grotesque*' to Cheon, Hauriou assigns to him also the adjectives of 'ridiculous' and 'comic'; one of which sounds to be a more critical judgement than the other. Perhaps, Hauriou's analysis nudges us towards the positive and negative duality – the *yin* and *yang* – of a person.

A monograph by H.C. Shea, entitled *Notes on Mrs Gunn's We of the Never Never* (c. 1940s), exposed many generations of school children to a certain set of attitudes and values. The racially stereotypical references expressed towards Australian Aborigines and the other Chinese cook, Sam Lee, were regrettable and may have been interpreted as tacit approval for the use of such terms. But in regard to Cheon, he wrote:

> Cheon, the Chinaman, was cook, gardener and general factotum at the station homestead. Fat in build, jovial in nature, he reminded the authoress of Shakespeare's creation – the merry, rollicking Sir John Falstaff ... The great moon-faced Asiatic cheerfully worked in the kitchen to give pleasure to the people on the station at Christmas-time.[12]

Even within these few sentences, Shea's disdain becomes apparent towards the character, Cheon, if not to the actual person who inspired the character. The combination of 'Chinaman', 'general factotum' and 'Asiatic [who] ... worked ... to give pleasure' calls to mind the

'Chinaman-cum-fawning servant' terminology of English-speaking condescension.

The themes of master–servant, bigotry and social class have also been addressed by Ouyang Yu in his article 'Lawson, Gunn and the "White Chinaman": A Look at How Chinese Are Made White in Henry Lawson and Mrs Aeneas Gunn's Writings' (2003).[13] Disapproval and shame seem to be implicit in Yu's use of the term 'white Chinaman', as if becoming such an entity meant that the Chinese sacrificed self-respect through subservient loyalty to a white boss, or, alternatively, that Chinese protagonists had to be transformed to make them more acceptable to white readers.[14] In regard to *We of the Never Never*, Yu argues that 'some of the qualities that appeal so much … [to Mr and Mrs Gunn about Cheon] … are at least those of a slave's or servant's …', with this dichotomy of master–servant or superior–inferior finding expression in Cheon's own behaviour towards the station Aborigines, for he is seen as being 'resolutely master-like in dealing with the blacks'.[15] Yu initially appears to classify *We of the Never Never* as fiction,[16] but, a few pages further on, he retreats from this somewhat by stating that the book is 'one of the rare factual accounts of life in the interior that at times reads like fiction'.[17] Lastly, Jeannie Gunn's seeming attempt to de-stereotype the Chinese cook impressed Yu.[18] For a work of early twentieth-century Australian non-fiction, such an endeavour was certainly worthy of mention.

Another publication that more or less reiterated the newspapers' published details about Cheon came from the research conducted by Iris ('Ira') Nesdale in *The Little Missus: Mrs Aeneas Gunn* (1977). Nesdale, responsible for a comprehensive study of Jeannie Gunn and her life, introduced Cheon in the first chapter of her book. Acknowledged as a 'loyal friend', Cheon and Jeannie Gunn continued to correspond after he left Australia in 1919, but despite Nesdale's having had privileged contact with Gunn's nieces and nephew, she seemed not to have uncovered any fresh information on Cheon or his cooking. Her reference to Gunn's own copy of *We of the Never Never*, containing the signatures of all the 'bush folk', apparently held by the La Trobe Library, State Library of Victoria, became a tantalising

Elsey homestead. Reproduced from *We of the Never Never* (1908).

exposé[19] until I attempted to gain access to it. Several library requests later, her claim has to be considered as incorrect.

Published only a few years after Nesdale, H.T. Linklater's *Echoes of the Elsey Saga* (1980) advanced Cheon's story, albeit incrementally. Although many of his claims have not been referenced, Linklater wrote that Cheon worked at Renner Springs cattle station during 1897 along with career stockman, Billy Miller.[20] As Billy Miller (or Billy Miller Linklater) was this author's uncle, it may be supposed that the stockman was the source of these anecdotes about Cheon. Linklater also added that Cheon worked on other stations in the Territory until advancing age, and what the cook called 'bluematics', had him booking a passage home.[21]

> He [Cheon] was held in the highest regard by the many who called at the station as they travelled through to distant parts of the great outback and many were the times they went on their way amply stocked with goodies from Cheon's kitchen ...[22]

And last but not least we come to Susanna De Vries' chapter, 'The Story Behind *We of the Never Never*', from her book *Great Pioneer Women of the Outback* (2005). This writer rendered a most refreshing representation of Cheon. True to the chapter title, De Vries satisfyingly provided details of the family backgrounds of both Aeneas Gunn and his wife-to-be, Jeannie Taylor; of their courtship; of their arrival in the Northern Territory and the Elsey; of Aeneas's death, Jeannie's return to Melbourne and, later, her death in 1961. Almost entirely absent from the account were depictions of the supposedly 'humorous' dialogue resulting from the attempts of non-English speakers to converse in that language. The enjoyment of reading De Vries' chapter flowed almost unhampered by what could be called racially influenced comic writing or racist terminology.

For a reader not yet familiar with *We of the Never Never*, De Vries has been seduced into embellishing the cook's clothing, describing him on arrival at Elsey Station as 'a fat jovial Chinaman dressed in a black-and-gold robe'.[23] Why she was provoked into 'orientalising' Cheon in this manner is a mystery, because, as far as can be determined from the *Never Never* text, he was dressed in 'tropical' whites as he dismounted from his horse on reaching his destination.

As the aforementioned H.T. Linklater has pointed out in his monograph, Cheon's career extended beyond his several months working at Elsey Station in the company of Aeneas and Jeannie Gunn. Astonishingly, Cheon's professional occupation linked his name with some of the most influential individuals in the Northern Territory. The chronology of these associations lent itself to formulating each of the succeeding chapters. Thus, Chapter 1 makes use of the small amount of early information identified about Cheon leading to his becoming a major celebrity through his immortalisation in *We of the Never Never* as well as his association with the 'whitest' man of the Territory. Chapter 2 explores what is known about Cheon and the 'great and good' man of Bradshaw's Run on the Victoria River. By Chapter 3, Cheon has taken up employment at Carlton Hill Station, near Wyndham, Western Australia, working for 'Hell-fire' Alf – Alfred Martin and his family.[24] After what appears to have been one of his visits to his own family in Guangdong, China, Cheon returns in Chapter 4 by accepting a position in the kitchen of the most politically powerful man in the Northern Territory at the time – His Excellency, the Administrator John Anderson Gilruth. In Chapter 5, Cheon is cooking for the Government Medical Officer, Dr Henry Leighton-Jones, and then, in Chapter 6, Cheon prepares meals for one of the wealthiest men of the Territory, Felix Ernest Holmes. Chapter 7 discusses Cheon's true identity and his connections in Hong Kong and with China, and by the Epilogue, we bid Cheon a fond and final adieu.

– ONE –

THE 'TIGER' MAN AND THE 'WHITEST' MAN TOGETHER

c. 1854 – c. 1903

Cheon, born a Tiger

Until information to the contrary comes to light, there is good reason to suppose that Hung Bak Cheong, otherwise known as Cheon, was born on 27 February 1854,[1] under the Chinese zodiac sign of the courageous Tiger. Doubtless, this would have pleased his parents, as this particular cosmology foretold of his becoming an honest man of importance and esteem. The Tiger, a *yang* sign, exhibits the robust energy normally associated with the masculine principle, and Tiger people are usually recognised by an aggressive yet unrefined element to their personalities, as well as by a preparedness to challenge others and equally to meet the challenges directed towards them. They enjoy being acknowledged as well as being considered ambitious, independent, determined, energetic, industrious and self-confident.[2]

Readers who are familiar with the characters in *We of the Never Never* will probably concede that the aforementioned description of a Tiger person comfortably accommodates Jeannie Gunn's depiction of Cheon. What makes her representation remarkable is that Gunn, presumably unacquainted with Chinese zodiac signs, used her own notes and observations of his behaviour to construct the character of Cheon. The words and actions of Cheon as described by her are astonishingly consistent with those that one might anticipate from a man born in a Tiger year.

When Cheon first appeared in the *Never Never* account, he made an arresting entrance for a character of short, portly stature. As the Elsey Station crowd was about to sit down to dinner, he caught their attention as 'a cloud of dust creeping along the horizon', metamorphosing into a 'huge mould of white jelly on horse-back' as he approached. As he drew ever closer to the homestead, the transformation continued.

> Directly it sighted us it rolled off the horse, whether intentionally or unintentionally we could not say, and leaving the beast to the care of chance, unfolded two short legs from somewhere and waddled towards us.

Still not finished with recounting Cheon's chameleon-like advance, Jeannie Gunn made another reference to his rotund figure, this time describing our hero as being 'like a ship's barrel in full sail'. With such a collection of comments directed at his chubby form, it is interesting to examine the earliest known photograph of Cheon, which reveals him to be a handsome, alert man, not yet in middle-age and with a bodily shape hardly reminiscent of a 'ship's barrel'. So, if phrases like 'huge mould of white jelly', 'rolled off the horse' and 'unfolded two short legs from somewhere and waddled towards us' are to be accepted as credible descriptions, the creation of this photograph must predate Cheon's taking up his position at Elsey Station. In 1902, when he and the Gunns came together, Cheon would have been close to middle-aged, being forty-eight years old, and by then, his physical appearance may have been a better match with the *Never Never* descriptions of him. Later photographs of Cheon, almost certainly taken between 1913 and 1919, visually reinforce those full-bellied descriptions.

Having reached the homestead verandah, Cheon wasted little time in demonstrating the traits of his Tiger personality. Parading unbridled self-confidence, he promptly announced himself to be their new station cook with established proficiencies in the kitchen, the garden and providing all that was necessary for a well-supplied household. In a few sentences, Jeannie Gunn captured the cook's nature and the value of his contribution – although her remark about his delightful disobedience was somewhat redolent of the indulgent tone of a master appraising a servant.

> Cheon's name was then formally entered in the station books as cook and gardener, at twenty-five shillings a week. That was the only vacancy he ever filled in the books, but in our life at the homestead he filled almost every other vacancy that required filling, and there were many.
>
> There was nothing he could not and did not do for our good; and it was well that he refused to be instructed in anybody's ways, for his own were delightfully disobedient and unexpected and entertaining.

While Cheon's claim on the imaginary title of Australia's first Chinese 'celebrity cook' dates from early twentieth century, his arrival in the Australian colonies and his budding reputation for fine cooking preceded any association with the Gunns. Jeannie Gunn asserted that Cheon arrived in the Territory in 1890,[3] but a War Precautions (Alien Registration) document (1916) referred to his much earlier arrival in Australia – during 1876. If the latter should be the case, Cheon would have been about twenty-two when he first landed either in the Northern Territory or in another colony of Australia. Nevertheless, it is believed that he was not among the first contingent of 187 Chinese Singaporeans recruited in 1874 to address the Northern Territory's manpower needs – a measure that turned out to be something of a labour fiasco.[4] Distinguishing himself from this disappointing batch of imported workers, Cheon – whatever the circumstances of his arrival – proved to be a godsend.

Cheon's pathway to celebrity

Before coming to Australia, Cheon spent substantial time working in California, amounting to almost a decade cooking in some of his earliest professional positions.[5] Thus, by the time he joined the staff of

Elsey Station, he was an experienced transnational traveller as well as an accomplished cook.

California's gold rush started in 1848, which was several years before Cheon was born. Nonetheless, news of the adventures and opportunities to be found overseas would have reached Cheon's home village. It was not unusual for older relatives or others to have joined these rushes, sending back to those at home stories of new and exciting lands across the ocean. Tales of 'hills ... made of silver and ... rivers [of] gold'[6] surely filled the daydreams of Chinese men and boys who were yet to experience the 'big golden mountain' for themselves. Roger Daniels, in his study on *Asian America* (1988), states that over 90 per cent of the Chinese in California were adult men;[7] however, it was not unknown for quite young boys to immigrate to gold rush countries, although they would usually be mentored or accompanied by older family members.[8] If Cheon had travelled to America when he was as young as twelve or thirteen, it would still have been in the aftermath of those earlier waves of hopeful seekers when he reached California.

In North America, Chinese who were not engaged in gold mining discovered that their labour was in demand in other domains. Elmer C. Sandmeyer, writing in *The Anti-Chinese Movement in California* (1991), observed that early Chinese arrivals to the west coast provided many of the personnel to California's food services. Thus, Chinese cooks fulfilled an important gap in the local labour market.

> Like all frontier communities, California experienced a pronounced scarcity of labor, which was accentuated by the rush to the gold fields. The Chinese were looked on as a veritable god-send. Women were very few, and the Chinese supplied the need for cooks, laundrymen, and the like, as well as that of the heavier work of the mines.[9]

Although the opportunities offered in California were seemingly advantageous to Cheon's career, the socio-political climate, during the years when he worked there, was not without volatility. Most probably, his time in America coincided with particular, well-known events of racial violence and the introduction of discriminatory legislation against Chinese.

From 1867 and for a number of decades afterwards, arguments against Chinese immigration became a feature of Californian politics. '[Political] parties vied with one another for the virulence of their anti-Chinese resolutions … and in publicly claiming credit for whatever restrictive laws and regulations were put into effect.'[10] Even so, the European attitude in the U.S.A. towards Chinese immigration contained contradictions, as it similarly did in Australia, with organised white labour advocating for the introduction of restrictions and employer organisations arguing against it.

> Labor justified its anti-immigrant attitudes chiefly by denying equal humanity to those it sought to exclude or expel. Some of the most attractive figures in the history of nineteenth century reform, such as Washington Gladden, had a blind spot insofar as the humanity of Chinese was concerned. Intellectuals from Ralph Waldo Emerson to E.A. Ross, politicians from John Quincy Adams to Theodore Roosevelt, all denied to Chinese most of the characteristics and attributes essential to humanity, or at least to white American humanity. Even those Protestant missionary clergy, who were in the late nineteenth century almost the sole public defenders of the Chinese, were distinctly halfhearted in their defense …[11]

What is not easy to discern is the effect, if any, of this exposure to racist condescension on the youthful Cheon. Perhaps, the thrill of adventure had greater impact than racial threats. In 1866 or thereabouts, California was still a dynamic destination, and for an adolescent away from the watchful eyes of his home village, the western Pacific coast offered a *Boys' Own* adventure full of opportunity, strange sights, a range of cross-cultural encounters, new flavours and other aromas. Cheon's Tiger nature could have been a vital component of his survival kit. The Central Pacific Railway was an employer of large numbers of Chinese workers who, besides the mundane tasks of laying railway tracks, undertook some spectacular and extraordinary feats of courage in order to do so. As well, Chinese settlement, labour and business acumen flourished in this new land regardless of the anti-Chinese agitation and the more worrisome menace of racial murder, such as the lynching of Chinese at Los Angeles in 1871.[12]

According to an article in the *Brisbane Courier* (1877), five special China-based companies recruited southern Chinese workers for

'California, Oregon and Nevada',[13] although some scholars refer to six companies.[14] The *Brisbane Courier* article claimed that the sixth company operated only in San Francisco, as a committee of management and arbitration for Chinese migrant labourers. Quite likely, one of these companies recruited the young Cheon. If this occurred when he was merely twelve years old, he may not have had the £100 payment to cover his expenses, meaning that he could have reached America in debt and with a bond to work off. Although bondsmanship imposed a certain loss of personal freedom, it was not completely negative, as the company in San Francisco supposedly housed, fed and made any necessary arrangements, especially for those with limited English language skills. This mentoring also extended to providing employment references. If an American household was offering a position – say, as a cook – the San Francisco-based company provided both a character reference and an assurance of good conduct for its candidate.[15] Although Cheon's working life was spent cooking primarily on the Californian goldfields,[16] could his position have been found in this way?

Before Cheon joined Elsey Station, there was one early reference to him in the Northern Territory, or maybe two, although the latter claim has to be considered uncorroborated. By 1897, Cheon was working at Renner Springs,[17] where it was difficult to imagine him fulfilling any other role than that of the station cook. Billy Miller (or Billy Miller Linklater) and Henry Peckham (later 'the Fizzer' in *We of the Never Never*) were also working at the same station, but handling the horses.

It was a remote location at which to discover Cheon at work, because the station was almost halfway to Alice Springs, and a long way from the any convenient coastal port by horse, dray or foot. It is intriguing to consider how he got there, for Cheon may not have been an enthusiastic equestrian. Jeannie Gunn noted that the only occasion she recalled Cheon's ever being seated atop a horse was the day of his arrival at the Elsey.[18] The former associate of Cheon, Billy Miller, appeared to have written little positive comment about Chinese people, although the sporadic, favourable mention proved the exception. In contrast, Henry Peckham appeared far less censorious. Given an opportunity to reunite at the Elsey, he and Cheon interacted warmly. For example, Peckham, as 'the Fizzer', announced to the station:

> 'Sore back here, fetch along the balsam. What ho, Cheon!' Cheon emerging greeted him as an old friend. 'Heard you were here. You're the boy for my money.'[19]

Having delivered his 'precious mail' into waiting hands at the station, he 'went to be entertained by Cheon',[20] as others went quiet, drifting away to consider their letters. In regard to Billy Miller – drover, poet, saddler and cook[21] – could it be that he viewed Cheon with the jealousy of a rival in their shared field of cooking? Miller, in his autobiographical writing, courteously acknowledged the other *Never Never* characters whom he encountered from time to time, but he neglected to mention ever having worked with Cheon or eaten his cooking, thus denying us one more historical memento.

Renner Springs (named after Dr Frederick Emil Renner, the medical officer in the early 1870s for the Overland Telegraph Line) gave its name to the nearby station. The station started breeding cattle, but after one of its previous managers, A.L. Prentice, became its new owner in 1900, the station diversified by adding not only more horses but also goats.[22] Renner Springs achieved a reputation for quality horses.[23] However, this reputation proved insufficient to keep the station operating. By 1904, with all its stock sold, Prentice took the decision to close down the station.[24] By then of course, Cheon too had moved on, having resigned in order to return to his home village in China in 1900 or thereabouts. On this trip, he returned not only to visit his family but to marry for the second time, since his first wife had died in childbirth. When we meet him in Jeannie Gunn's reminiscence, he has only just left the arms of his new wife to pursue his transnational existence between Australia and China. It is impossible to claim categorically that the passenger records to Darwin show Cheon's return to the Territory, but among a handful of entries of interest there is one, in particular, which indicates that an 'Ah Cheon', aged forty, entered Darwin during October 1901 as a passenger on board the *Chingtu*. However, in 1901 our Cheon would have been forty-seven years old.

The second and more tenuous reference involved a Chinese hotel cook at the Katherine. A few years before Cheon was linked to Renner Springs Station, Tom Pearce (later 'Mine Host' in *We of the Never Never*) took over the licence for the Sportsman Hotel at the Katherine from its original licensee, Bernard Murphy.[25] In 1894, this hotel was considered noteworthy because of its copious fare prepared by an unnamed but excellent Chinese cook.[26] But it has been impossible to identify this excellent Chinese cook from existing records. According to Jeannie Gunn, Cheon would have been recognised by 'most Territorians'.[27] If this were so, it is probable that he worked in settings of high exposure, such as the dining room of a well-patronised public house, which the Sportsman Hotel purported to be. Not only was Cheon indeed readily recognised by Thomas Wakelin ('Little Johnny', the carpenter, in *We of the Never Never*), as the cook was advancing on the Elsey homestead, but Wakelin and Henry Peckham could hardly believe their good fortune to have Cheon cooking for them at the Elsey. Because of the enthusiasm of their reception for him, might it be that the unnamed excellent Chinese cook of the Sportsman Hotel was our Cheon?

The 'whitest' man: Aeneas Gunn

With their married life merely a few weeks old, having celebrated their nuptials on 31 December 1901, Aeneas and Jeannie Gunn arrived at Darwin by ship from Melbourne on 16 January 1902, eventually reaching Elsey Station in early February. There Aeneas was to take up his responsibilities as the new station manager.[28] Although Aeneas had been working as a librarian at Prahran, in Melbourne, before his marriage, he was no novice to the Territory, having already enjoyed a number of north Australian adventures. In 1890, he participated in an expedition led by his cousin, Joseph Bradshaw, whose plan had been to set up of a homestead at the Kimberley, in Western Australia. The highs and lows of this venture subsequently served as the basis for a series of twenty-four articles written by Aeneas Gunn and published in various Melbourne suburban newspapers – the *Prahran Telegraph*, *St Kilda Advertiser* and *Malvern Argus* – between May and November 1899.[29]

But the Kimberley enterprise collapsed, and Joseph Bradshaw turned his attention to the Northern Territory, where he took up a forty-two-year pastoral lease in 1894.[30] Aeneas acquired his knowledge of the Territory while working for his cousins at Bradshaw's Run, on the Victoria River, and through his friendship and association with Alfred Searcy, appointed by the South Australian Government as the Sub-Collector of Customs for the Northern Territory. Aeneas Gunn accompanied his friend Searcy on a number of excursions to places along the northern Australian coastline.

One interesting aspect of this friendship was its muscular compatibility. Born in 1854, Alfred Searcy married Jane Annette Rainsford in 1876, but during 1890 – for health reasons seemingly precipitated by the tropical climate – his wife and family left Darwin and returned to Adelaide.[31] As a result, Searcy was managing on his own when he struck up an acquaintance with the then unmarried Aeneas Gunn. Although Searcy was the older by eight years, the two men presented as having similar interests – especially towards people in general – and both were keen to satisfy an adventurous curiosity and wrote about these events. As birds-of-a-feather, they arguably were perceived as men of reasonable temperament.

However, the thorny situations with which they were forced to deal taunted them. For example, Searcy as a government officer had to administer the Customs law and adhere to its racialist culture against non-Anglo-Celtic settlers, including the Chinese. On departing Darwin, all Chinese had their luggage searched meticulously for undeclared gold, whereas, in the absence of specific intelligence indicating otherwise, a European's declaration was accepted unquestioningly.[32] But as an individual, Searcy was a well-known advocate for Chinese labour[33] and the talent of Chinese cooks,[34] and he further much admired the style and honesty of the Chinese merchant class – an admiration that was, most likely, mutual.[35] The New Year wishes from the Man Fung Lau (or in Mandarin, Wàn Fâng Lo establishment was an example of the many tributes that Searcy received from the influential members of Darwin's Chinese community.[36] Similarly, while Aeneas Gunn was working at Bradshaw's Run, it became a part of his duty to scare off people whom we now refer to as the 'traditional owners' of the land. The Aboriginal tribes who inhabited the coastal lands near Bradshaw's lease were well known for their fierce aggressiveness, so this pre-emptive action might have been perceived by some as a safety precaution. Searcy was sympathetic towards his 'dear old chum' for having to grapple with such a predicament. While this piece of Aeneas Gunn's writing was cited as an illustration of northern mangrove swamps, it also documented a conducted hunt on other human beings. Searcy's prefatory remarks from *In Northern Seas* (1905) stated: 'For the safety of the station he was on, poor old Gunn had to go out and kill something'. Aeneas wrote about his experience as follows:

> We had not gone very far when we startled a pheasant from its noontide nap in one of the isolated clumps of trees … The blacks, who are almost preternaturally keen in detecting any abnormality in the natural effect surrounding them, were, doubtless, instantly on the alert, for, although we waited long in the hiding the trees assured us, we had hardly commenced to move from cover when we saw several dusky figures running across the salt marsh into the mangroves. We started in pursuit at a run, but when we reached the camp we found it, as we expected deserted … We did not then wait … but, picking up the tracks of the retreating savages, followed them into the mangroves. The successful pursuit … in such a tangle of roots and branches was almost as hopeless of achievement as the proverbial search for a needle in a stack of hay; but the chagrin we felt over the defeat of our previous purpose fired our spirits with restless zeal, and each selecting a track, we followed the diverging footmarks through the dense, dark, eerie, smelling inferno, with the instinct of sleuth hounds. Nothing will ever obliterate from my memory the impressions that hunt made on my mind … But there was a track in the mud, a purpose in my heart, which did not become less insistent as every now and then on ahead I could hear a crack, the sound of a branch pushed aside, and its swishing swing back into place …[37]

Not too long after this episode, Aeneas's health failed, necessitating his return to Melbourne in 1895.[38] Yet, neither facing danger nor wretched experience appeared to have left any lasting dent on his generally positive attitude towards life or, given the choice, on the gentlemanly manner with which he chose to deal with others or with situations that he encountered. Aeneas Gunn's *vale*, published by the *Prahran Telegraph* (1903), supports this assertion by describing his principal qualities as follows:

> Mr Gunn was a gentleman, who, by his genial nature endeared himself to all he came into contact with and beyond this he was a gentleman of considerable culture and with a strong sympathetic insight into literary matters. He was the best class of Bohemian, and his superficial faults ever leaned to virtue's side … He had spent some of his early life in the north, and the fatal fascination of the tropics never left him. His heart always turned thither, to the land of the Never Never, to wild and primitive nature.[39]

A favourable assessment of Aeneas Gunn also resonated from the pages of *We of the Never Never*. Lee Ken, whose worsening health while *en route* to Daly Waters Station for work had brought him to the Elsey to die, was so appreciative of the compassionate reception that Aeneas Gunn offered him that he praised 'the "good boss", who treated all men alike', and in a similar vein, another traveller who was seventy years old and whose own poor health forced him to accept Elsey care and hospitality considered Aeneas to be the 'whitest' man that he had ever known.[40] This elderly guest required considerable monitoring. He stretched Jeannie Gunn's patience to the limit, through his trying behaviour and by demanding that Cheon prepare 'impossible dishes' for him.[41]

Nonetheless, Aeneas Gunn's accolade of the 'whitest' man has been credited to this old – possibly eccentric – man who wanted to acknowledge the kindnesses shown him by paying a compliment to the boss of the Elsey. Use of the term 'whitest' man carries its own 'tribal' history with it. Some writers have claimed that, even with diligent effort, it was difficult to disassociate its use from racialist thinking connected with skin colour and notions of white racial superiority. However, this was not an impossibility. In the case of Aeneas Gunn, such a tribute highlighted his magnanimity and humanitarianism – qualities that made him outstanding, irrespective of race or skin colour.

Cheon connects with the 'whitest' man

Having had considerable North American and Australian exposure to the ways of Europeans, Cheon showed little reservation in expressing his candid opinion on all kinds of matters at the Elsey, including his thoughts on the 'whitest' man, despite the latter's also being the boss. Nonetheless, the relationship between Cheon and Aeneas Gunn started amicably enough and apparently finished in a similar fashion, despite a few rough patches along the way. Not only was Cheon born in the Year of the Tiger, but so too was Aeneas's chum, Searcy. Based on Chinese zodiac predictions, a strong likelihood existed that the compatibility between Aeneas and Searcy might similarly have developed between Cheon and his boss, in the form of a good working relationship.

After the introductions had been concluded, the new station cook said that he would have a seat, and his new boss – the 'whitest' man – laughingly replied, 'Please yourself!' Cheon certainly pleased himself, soon taking control of the household staff – the station women, the

Aboriginal men (Jimmy, Billy Muck, Rejected) and everyone else – as well as the practical operation of the homestead and garden. When Aboriginal Jimmy's 'mock' challenge to this new, yet jovial, 'controller' provoked Cheon's 'arms and legs to fly out' towards Jimmy, every witness to the event was taken by surprise.[42] This technique described by Jeannie Gunn as an 'infuriated Chinese Catherine-wheel' is probably the only reference to Chinese martial art technique in any piece of early Australian writing.

Whether the intentional or unintentional challenge took a physical or social form, Cheon rose to meet it. Evening banter with other men at the station produced this illustration of Cheon's drollness, as allegedly recollected by Jack McLeod (the 'Quiet Stockman' in *We of the Never Never*):

> There was this one chap by the name of Paddy. He used to come every three months with mail and goods in a … four horse and … spring trolley. Well, he's stopped there over night and he used to tease the life out of this Chinese chap. They called him Cheon.
>
> One night there they was all sitting around the fire and they was teasing him, and this Paddy said to him, 'Cheon, how is it you don't get cross and nasty with us, the way I tease you?' And this Chinese chap said to him, 'No', he says, 'Cheon don't get cross. Cheon's a very placid man. It takes a lot to upset Cheon, but me tell you, when you stop teasing Cheon, Cheon stop peeing in the soup.' (laughs)[43]

With his martial art skills, his redoubtable prowess with the shotgun – used to supply wild duck for the homestead – and above all his wry humour, Cheon established his position as someone not to get offside with to any serious extent. After all, he was a man born in a Tiger year!

From the pages of the *Never Never*, it becomes steadily established that Cheon and Jeannie Gunn enjoyed their own special relationship. As her senior by a couple of decades, Cheon might have felt fatherly or protective towards her and may have thought that she was 'wasted on an Englishman',[44] and she, in her way, seems to have been delighted and amused by his outlook, his idiosyncratic language and his enthusiasm for life. It was not the kind of relationship that Jeannie Gunn and Sam Lee, the station's cook at the time of her arrival, shared. Sam Lee was not without abilities – being a cook, gardener and saddler among other things

– so the friction between him and the new mistress arose largely from incompatibility, and not so much from the cook's lack of ability. During the early months of their association when everything was fresh, Jeannie Gunn's opinion was positive, considering Sam Lee to be a treasure.[45]

After departing the Elsey, Sam Lee continued as a cook, last working at the Ord River Station.[46] Initially, Aeneas Gunn shared his wife's assessment of Sam Lee. Soon after the Gunns first reached the Elsey as husband and wife, Aeneas, referring to Sam Lee, wrote to his brother, Bob, that they had 'an excellent cook'.[47] Had there not been those interactional problems between the new mistress and Sam Lee, Cheon might not have been summonsed to the Elsey, and thus, the *Never Never* story would have been without one of its favourite characters.

Despite developing a protective attitude towards Jeannie Gunn, it became apparent that Cheon at first considered the boss's wife to be of small value in the station's garden and hopeless with the household staff.[48] However, Jeannie Gunn's homemade, fly-proof dining tent had Cheon 'chuckling' and her eventual success in the house garden,[49] had him favourably reappraising the negativity of his earlier assessment.[50] As was his nature, Cheon took an interest in many matters concerning the homestead. When he thought that repairs to the homestead building needed to be stepped up, he 'daily and hourly' tried to encourage Thomas Wakelin to increase his efforts[51] as well as enlist Dave Suttie's assistance (Dan, the head stockman, of *We of the Never Never*) whenever the latter could be spared from herding the stock.[52]

Cheon's discontent with the 'whitest' man surfaced over Jeannie's having to patch her daily attire regularly while waiting for her luggage to arrive at the Elsey from Melbourne. Cheon 'openly disapproved of this state of affairs',[53] and considered that the boss had failed in his spousal duty to provide for his wife as a good husband should. On another occasion, when Cheon learned that the boss and the mistress were merely sojourning for a couple of days at the homestead after a lengthy period of droving, he 'hinted darkly that the Maluka [Aeneas Gunn] was not a fit and proper person to be entrusted with the care of a woman, and suggested that he should undertake to treat the missus as she should be treated…'[54] But, when the circumstances changed and Jeannie Gunn was forced to remain in residence at the homestead, Cheon had a complete reversal of opinion.

Such criticisms were apparently momentary and any consequential tension evaporated just as quickly. However, it took Jeannie Gunn's struggle with a bout of influenza to cement a bond between the 'whitest' man and the 'Tiger' man. Nursing her back to good health proved a unifying experience, through which 'the Maluka and Cheon … won each other's undying regard because of their treatment of the missus'.[55] Whether a form of rivalry or competition affected their former interaction can only be guessed, but with Jeannie Gunn regaining her health though their joint efforts, Aeneas Gunn and Cheon moved forward with their own relationship.

Unfortunately, not a single recipe specifically used by Cheon survives as a testament to his culinary prowess. Thus, it is impossible to verify the flavour or the quality of his cooking, yet while that is the situation, neither has there been the least suggestion that his meals were regarded as disappointing or unappetising. At the Elsey, in addition to the daily routine of feeding two or three meals each day to the station population, with sponge cakes and scones as special offerings, Cheon demonstrated a competency at invalid cookery, and more famously at preparing a sumptuous Christmas fare.

The splendid Christmas table of 1902 inspired Aeneas Gunn to praise Cheon effusively in a Boxing Day letter addressed to his aunt, Margaret Bradshaw. In her nephew's experience of Christmases past, Cheon's fare had never been bettered. Aeneas's assessment of Cheon's culinary excellence rated him as more than just another Chinese cook – indeed as the finest chef in an open field, despite being handicapped by a restricted range of kitchen utensils.

> Ah Cheon covered himself in glory by the excellence of his viands. No white cook with the same limited appliances could have made so grand a show. I have never and never want to sit down to a better dinner anywhere. The king of the feast was certainly the bland, the beaming, the bright, the cheerful, the irrepressible and the irresistible Ah Cheon. He is a masterpiece, a wonder and I am beginning to get suspicious of him for his marvellous excellence. Our guests departed full men and happy with innocent fullness and happiness – hop beer was our strongest tonic, and Ah Cheon and the Missus (the real organisers of the spread) are happy because everyone else was happy.[56]

Perhaps, Cheon's boiled Christmas pudding recipe might be fabricated by using another boiled pudding recipe which could be modified with sufficient eggs, port wine, almonds and raisins to match Cheon's mixture.[57] Similarly, Cheon's Christmas ham, after being boiled in water for several hours, would have been rested before some of the skin was removed to expose the fat. The exposed ham fat may have been scored in a diamond-shaped criss-crossed manner before being dressed with layer of breadcrumbs and baked in a slow oven until golden brown.[58] Besides the other fare including Christmas cake, fruit mince pies,[59] soup, roast vealer, cauliflower, peas, beans, tomatoes, sweet potatoes, bread sauce, sweets, cakes and fruit,[60] it might have been that the roasted, brown chickens achieved their colour by being seasoned with a marinade that contained oil and soya sauce.

In regard to invalid cookery with which he aided Jeannie Gunn's recovery from influenza, Cheon was known to have prepared rice water, chicken jelly, barley water, egg flips, beef tea, junket 'and every invalid food he had ever heard of'.[61] The rice water could been a favoured Chinese recipe prepared by slowly boiling round grain rice in water until it forms a thickened, opaque soup, which then might be pressed through a sieve to make its consistency finer and uniform. This soup (known as *bak jook* in Cantonese or *bái zhōu* in Mandarin) might be served sweetened or savoury to feed the ailing.

There is little evidence that Jeannie Gunn was enthusiastic about cooking herself, so there was every possibility that she and Cheon were not rivals for the kitchen domain. As a consequence, the method and ingredients that Cheon used to prepare the station's meals may have received only her token attention. Her main enjoyment was in the partaking, not in how the food was prepared. Even though Cheon's dishes cannot be duplicated by recipe, it would seem that those who had the good fortune to dine at his table were well satisfied. Alfred Searcy, during his time in the Northern Territory, developed a burgeoning reputation as a food connoisseur, tasting all kinds of tropical fruit[62] and wild seafood dishes[63] among other unusual meats. Some of this fare eaten by Searcy had been prepared by Chinese chefs, but it cannot be determined if he partook of our Cheon's cooking. Had he done so, Searcy's review would have provided highly valuable and independent comment. Alfred Searcy returned to Adelaide himself in 1896 and did not revisit the Territory during the remaining years while Cheon was still a resident there.

As a concluding comment, it would be elating to be able to claim that Aeneas and Jeannie Gunn were absolutely innocent of using pejorative racial terms throughout the entirety of their writings, but it cannot be. Nevertheless, they were still exceptional individuals in the hyper-racial climate of early twentieth-century Australia. Aeneas's treatment of the variety of people who came into his life was largely tempered by kindness and generosity.

As for Jeannie Gunn, it is inexplicable that her writing did not attract significant condemnation from others with more extreme racial views. Those who championed causes supporting or promoting the position of non-whites attracted attention and comment. As illustration, Alfred Searcy's advocacy for Chinese labour in the tropics was still remembered even in his obituary in 1925. It may be argued that Jeannie Gunn in *We of the Never Never* gave Aboriginal and Chinese characters a certain voice and definite agency – aspects of expression not so readily found in other contemporary writing. Her Aboriginal and Chinese characters do not appear as just mere racial subordinates or a source of labour, even if she was unable to sustain this position continuously. Jeannie Gunn also rescued the little Euro-Aboriginal girl, Bett Bett, known as Dolly, and enjoyed a genuine, cross-racial friendship with Cheon that flourished for more than two decades.

– TWO –

CHEON AT BRADSHAW'S RUN, VICTORIA RIVER

c. 1906 – c. 1909

The death of Aeneas Gunn from malarial dysentery in early March 1903 and the return of Jeannie Gunn to Melbourne, soon thereafter, brought to an end the salad days for the Elsey Station personalities. The station population had been grief-stricken by its boss's death and, although no individual mourner was singled out for mention, Cheon grieved along with the rest. After the burial service, Jeannie seemed to find some solace in sharing her observations with her brother-in-law.

> It is all over & if you had been here you would have thanked your brother's men for the heart whole service in his memory. It was pathetically touching & has made a bond between me and these rough men that nothing can break – I have never heard before great strong men sobbing their hearts out & it did me good

> to feel that everyone loved him – The kindly simple blacks came down & asked to be permitted to draw the buggy with my Maluka [Aeneas] upon it to the little cemetery upon the hill – Their looks of sorrow & love were very touching …[1]

Following the committal of their boss's body to the ground, it would not have been beyond the realms of possibility for several of the men to have taken a shot of strong drink to dull their sensibilities. Cheon might have desired some kind of balm, too, for despite being in deep mourning, he and his kitchen may have remained at the ready to prepare a suitable wake – a ritual understood in both English and southern Chinese cultures. The cook felt a great fondness for Aeneas Gunn and, as the latter's death followed soon after that of another at the Elsey – Lee Ken – Cheon's anguish could well have been amplified.

> Lee Ken was riding from Darwin to cook at Daly Waters, when he became sick, on [Chinese] New Year's Eve, 1903. He died on February 18.
>
> Ah Cheon, our cook, was in a terrible state. As it was his New Year Festival he would not touch the body, or he would have to return to China for purification. But he wanted Lee Ken buried properly. So he told The Maluka what to do and then threw charms and special glass bracelets into the grave, saying: 'Lee Ken, you're dead. Go on, go on, and you'll come to …' He muttered something and then turned to us … 'I've told him where to do!'
>
> How pleased Ah Cheon was that we buried Lee Ken in new pyjamas. He would be received with deference, not as a beggar, if he had been left in travel-stained clothes. The Maluka read the Christian Burial Service after Ah Cheon had finished.[2]

Cheon becomes part of the Bradshaw enterprise

With Jeannie Gunn having bid her poignant adieu to the Elsey, presumably station life gradually reverted to a more familiar rhythm, yet it was not the same as before. Thus, Cheon no longer announced the station meal times cheerfully, calling to the boss and the mistress along with the others to come and eat.[3] Plausibly, Cheon continued cooking at the Elsey for another year or two, before he too departed, returning to China during 1905 for a period to be with his own family. From Jeannie Gunn's own notes, it is believed that 'on his return [Cheon] dictated a letter … through

Mr Joseph Bradshaw, Victoria River, where he was then cooking'.[4] The contents of this letter indicated that regular contact occurred between Cheon and Joseph Bradshaw.

> Not the least hearty welcome was that extended to me by good old Cheon. Now let me tell you that when I presented him with that most useful present, the combination knife that you so thoughtfully sent to him with his own name in the immortal language enamelled on it, his eyes (and every feature) gazed spellbound – and at last his whole face evolved into a most genial smile, and he expressed his many thanks to you in many different forms.
>
> Hardly a day passes without him making some reference to you. He is giving me a Canton dime to give to you to blunt the hyperbolical edge of the knife that might cut friendship. Cheon desires me to tell you that his two daughters are quite well, also the son he purchased for 200 dollars. Also that his wife is now 32 years old.[5]

Joe Bradshaw was the undisputed leader of the Bradshaw adventures to the Kimberley, Western Australia, and to the Victoria River, Northern Territory, with his brothers and his cousin, Aeneas Gunn, happily following along. During their boyhood in Victoria, the die had already been cast on their adventurous and generally decent natures. The Bradshaw and Gunn boys published their own hand-drawn newspaper called *The Mischief*, in which a youthful voice expressed the sentiments that become the template for their adult years.

> *The Mischief* paper you should get;
> For it tells you all that is new.
> And five thousand pounds I will bet
> That, all that it tells you, is true.
>
> Men, should be honest, truthfull, just,
> And upright, that is my belief.
> And all of these, confess you must;
> Are to be found, in the *Mischief*.
>
> Men, should be large, and go about:
> Just like the *Mischief*, great, and good,

> Go anywhere, you will find him out.
> If you did not want to, you would.[6]

If the year 1903 contained devastating events for the Taylor and Gunn families, then 1905 turned out to be correspondingly horrific for their Bradshaw relatives. With Joe Bradshaw travelling to Britain on business, his brother Fred Bradshaw undertook the everyday management of their station on his own. Fred, in correspondence with their other brother John, based in Melbourne, repeatedly lamented Joe's absence, bemoaning the dilemmas involved in attempting to resolve particular matters. Before his departure, Joe Bradshaw had employed another stockman, named Webster, apparently without consulting Fred, and this engagement was not working out. Further, their vessels plying the Bradshaw route from Wyndham via Darwin to Borroloola continuously required maintenance, repairs and replacement parts.

Adding even more to his vexation, Fred remarked that he had to dismiss their Chinese cook, during June 1905, although he had been a member of staff for a long time. Fred believed that the cook was 'too fond of selling grog on the sly and pilfering from the store'. The cook and gardener at Bradshaw's Run until early 1901 was Ah Wah,[7] but by 1902, natural attrition saw the station's cooking taken up by a man called Ah Tong.[8] These incidental details support the prospect that the discharged cook was him. As a replacement, Fred Bradshaw[9] engaged a European cook named C.J. Williams.[10] But, more devastating events were still to come.

In November 1905, the news arrived via Hong Kong that Joe Bradshaw was on his way home to the Northern Territory on board the SS *Eastern*, which was expected to berth at Darwin by 9 December.[11] He was returning triumphant, as his business trip to Britain had been a success, securing an agreement from the Eastern, African and Cold Storage Company to invest under his managerial guidance a 'half-million pounds of English capital' towards the development of Arnhem Land.[12]

In order to rendezvous with Joe at Darwin, Fred Bradshaw set off from Bradshaw's Run on the launch *Bolwarrah* on 12 November.[13] The plan was that the brothers, once reunited, would return to the station together for Christmas.[14] But this did not happen, as near Cape Scott, all the white men – Fred Bradshaw, Ivan Egeroffe, Jeremiah Skeahan and young Ernest

Dannock – were murdered by a group of Aborigines, native to the Port Keats district.[15] Bobby, one of the four original Aboriginal crew from Victoria River who were also on board the *Bolwarrah*, provided the details of the catastrophe. The whole misadventure started while the launch was anchored at the Government Bore at Port Keats, where Fred Bradshaw had gone ashore. At this point, three of the original Aboriginal crew decided to flee, while supposedly searching for a dilly bag lost during an earlier expedition to locate some fresh water. The Aboriginal crew was fearful of the coastal Aborigines.

With the purpose of replacing the lost crew members, Fred Bradshaw and Ernie Dannock proceeded to round up four coastal Aborigines. This enabled the *Bolwarrah* to up anchor and sail on until nightfall. Because the four coastal Aborigines had been taken against their will, they were tied up to prevent their escape but also in a manner that made it difficult for them to achieve any sleep. On the next day, the launch set off again, but the engine broke down at about dusk. The shanghaied crew members were untied and fed along with everyone else. With a misplaced sense of goodwill, everyone on board settled down for the night, but in the darkness, the white men were attacked and killed. Bobby from the Victoria River was tossed overboard during the mêlée, aiding his getaway and thus allowing him to raise the alarm by 8 December.

The missing launch drifted to a beach about four miles south of Cape Scott. Fred Bradshaw's body was located that Christmas Day, as were those of the other three passengers.[16]

At Darwin, Joe Bradshaw had been awaiting the arrival of the *Bolwarrah*, but before too long, the circumstances behind his brother's non-appearance became known.

Presumably, the circumstances of Fred's death were communicated by Joe Bradshaw through his private correspondence ahead of what was published in Australia's newspapers. How the other members of the Bradshaw family and Jeannie Gunn reacted to the news has to be imagined.

In September 1906, another of the Bradshaws' vessels, the *Wai Hoi*, carried a cargo of coffins for the murder victims of Cape Scott. Joe Bradshaw's intention was to transfer his brother's remains to Bradshaw's Run for a final reinterment. Even though certain burial arrangements still had to be finalised, there was some indication that Joe was again beginning to get on with his life following the loss of his brother. He and Mr C.J. Chambers, honorary secretary of the Victoria River Racing Club, hosted a 'pleasant' luncheon at the Victoria Hotel, enjoyed by several other prominent members of the North Australia League. It was a social occasion without solemnity, according to the local newspaper. Joe Bradshaw proposed a toast to the president, Mr E.V.V. Brown, that 'was received with musical honours, and was followed by others, including the health of the hostess of the Hotel Victoria, Mrs E. Ryan, which was received with great enthusiasm, and was responded to by two chivalrous gentlemen present'.[17]

The working relationship between Cheon and Joe Bradshaw may have begun in 1906, but by 1907, this association had become distinctly robust. The tone of Joe Bradshaw's letter to Jeannie Gunn about Cheon's reaction to her gift of a combination knife serves as the prime resource for this information. The opening sentence indicates that Cheon welcomed Joe's return to Bradshaw's Run, and Joe's reference to 'good old Cheon' suggested a mutual cordiality. While the timing of this event can only be conjectured, perhaps Cheon had taken possession of his gift some time after mid-May 1907, when Joseph eventually returned to Victoria River after a restorative visit to his family in Melbourne, where he also delivered a talk to the Royal Geographical Society on the Northern Territory, as well as carrying out other duties.[18]

In *We of the Never Never*, Cheon's energy and enthusiasm for cooking received due praise, but the outcome of his gardening efforts depended on a number of factors. The dry, hot weather, lack of easily accessible water, abundance of pests and communal tending to the station's garden were all considerations. Nonetheless, the agricultural accomplishments of himself, Jeannie Gunn, Billy Muck, Rejected and others, should not be disregarded. Just before Christmas 1902, the Elsey garden promised rock melons, watermelons, marrows, cucumbers, sweet potatoes and bananas.[19] Reports existed claiming that agricultural efforts nearer to the coast paid better dividends. At Borroloola, on the east coast of the Territory, Chinese enterprise guaranteed a good supply of fresh produce for the local community,[20] and apparently, at Bradshaw's Run on the Victoria River, the growing conditions and exploitable water resources also suited Chinese agricultural practices.

When Senator Story toured the Victoria River in July 1907, he was especially impressed with Bradshaw's Run, which had become something of a farming showpiece. The *Brisbane Courier* reported Senator Story claiming:

> One thing that struck me was the vegetable garden at Bradshaw's station. They kept a Chinese cook, and there was seen to be growing every vegetable product that could be found in the Southern parts of the Commonwealth, proving that with irrigation the country will grow anything ... At Bradshaw's station they had a pipe from One Spring Hills from which they irrigated a large portion of land. Most of the people seemed hopeful regarding future prospects.[21]

Although the identity of the Chinese cook was undisclosed in the report, our Cheon – cook and gardener – was working at Bradshaw's Run during the time of the senator's tour. Irrigation, Cheon's industry and passion, and Joe Bradshaw's adventuresome, entrepreneurial spirit and interest in botanical specimens all combined there to make the property's vegetable garden a noteworthy enterprise.

Regardless of tragedy or setback, Joe Bradshaw remained committed to promoting the Northern Territory. In addition to his campaigning for investment and his public speaking in favour of the Territory, his vice-presidency of the North Australia League (NAL) was another example of his passion. The NAL adopted positions that did not endorse Asiatic advancement in the Territory, even though the Chinese contribution to the agricultural, commercial and mining sectors was highly significant, as indeed were Cheon's efforts at Bradshaw's Run. Was it possible that Joe Bradshaw was not of same mind with some of the other members of the NAL?

The thrust of his talk to the Royal Geographical Society neither ignored nor downplayed the significance of Chinese contribution in the Territory.[22] From the moment of their arrival at Darwin harbour, according to Joe Bradshaw, a passenger could readily appreciate the Chinese participation in the local community. He declared that Chinese porters were ready to take charge of a passenger's luggage at call,[23] and the visitor or returning traveller to Darwin would enter the township thus:

> A small turnstile at the top of the hundred steps admits the traveller to the broad streets of the town, covered with red dust, or in the wet weather red mud, and in the Chinese quarter flanked by endless rows of corrugated iron tenements. Proceeding into the European quarter we find the streets better made, and kept in finer order. The houses and stores are detached, some are built of freestone, and surrounded with ornamental trees … The leading Chinese Temple is open day and night to all comers, and on bronze and brazen altars, the daily sacrifice burns without intermission.[24]

His presentation provided a description of Darwin by night, which offered shopping and social entertainment for residents and visitors alike. For his audience of Melburnians, constrained by a culture of 'early closing', this prospect may have seemed highly exotic, or even nostalgic, and enchanting. Darwin's Chinese community had been instrumental in making much of this happen, including the cultivation of a local supply of fresh produce grown successfully in selected sections of what was generally held to be dubious agricultural terrain.

> [T]he streets in the Asiatic quarters of the town are rendered lively at night time by the crews from the boats … Occasionally the police also have a lively evening in preserving order and peace between the many eastern nationalities that congregate in the bazaars and booths. But it must not be imagined that the town is a disorderly one as the reverse is the case, indeed considering the great admixture of eastern and island races that form its labouring population, it is the most regular and law abiding seaport town in existence. Inspector Waters, who is chief of the Police, and his staff are worthy of compliment for the efficient and unobtrusive manner in which the peace and respectability of the place are maintained during both day and night. Ladies from the European quarter can walk through the streets and stalls of Chinatown at all hours and receive nothing but deferential attention. The trades are nearly all run by Chinese. Tailoring is essentially one of their professions … There are numerous shops for the disposal of fruit and vegetables, some of which are imported from the east, and from southern Australia, but the larger quantity is locally grown. The land on which the town is situated consists chiefly of ironstone grit lying on a freestone base, and is not by any means fertile, but numerous valleys and basins that intersect it are rich enough to grow anything, and are occupied by the industrious

> [Chinese], without whose presence in this part of the Commonwealth the white Australian would fare badly in the matter of fresh food.[25]

His closing – yet possibly most important – comment highlighted that aspect of the Northern Territory society which contested the racial monotony of White Australia. His description of the poly-ethnic crowd, doing nothing out of the ordinary other than farewelling friends or boarding a carriage at the Darwin Railway Station, might be appreciated by some as a precursor of the multicultural Australia that had not yet formally come about.

> The railway station is a busy centre on two mornings and two evenings each week. There the white, black, yellow and brown of the population often come in considerable numbers to see their friends off, or to go off themselves.[26]

Joseph Bradshaw and the North Australian League

Without question, Joe Bradshaw's enthusiasm for the Northern Territory existed well before the initial meeting of the North Australian League in May 1901.[27] This meeting was an attempt to revamp the regional progress association, the earlier version of which – the Northern Territory Reform Association – had been established in 1883.[28]

> The formation of an Association to be called the North Australian League is without doubt a move in the right direction, and if people throughout the country will only co-operate heartily in rendering the League a thoroughly strong and representative body, it should, by working in harmony with the similar association formed south, be enabled to bring a considerable pressure to bear in forcing the attention of the powers that be to a more serious consideration of the various questions affecting our welfare. In the general scramble and keen competition for existence, it is a suicidal policy to sit still and fold one's hands, and the same truism has an even closer application with regard to public affairs … The need of some such association has long been recognised, and it is to be sincerely hoped the new League may have a long lease of life, and justify its existence by useful and vigorous action. The objects of the League may be considered rather ambitious, but equally important results have often accrued from even humbler beginnings; and

> if members will only sink petty jealousies and work unitedly, it is difficult to set a limit to the good the League may accomplish.[29]

However, in 1901, Australia was besotted with nationalism and rightly or wrongly preoccupied with racial exclusion – a social agenda from which the Northern Territory was not exempt. The NAL had been proactive in petitioning its members against issuing any further mining licences or leases to Asians. The League was responding to the concern of the South Australian Government, which believed that uncontrolled continuation of the practice might negatively affect the Federal Government's attitude to assuming responsibility for the Territory.[30] Local enthusiasm for the NAL continued for many months, especially in regard to its efforts of linking remote branches with the main branch and with its promotion of the Territory to prospective financial investors.[31]

In 1902, Joe Bradshaw, as vice-president and provisional honorary secretary of the Melbourne branch of the NAL, wrote from Melbourne to the League in the Northern Territory seeking advice on three issues: whether to endorse the Australian proposal to take over British New Guinea; whether Asian labour was essential for the advancement of tropical Australia; and whether support existed for the exclusion of Asians and other non-whites from Australia. In response to the New Guinea proposal, the NAL formally offered no opinion, swayed by discussion at the meeting that a negative response from itself to this matter might backfire on it when the time arrived for the Commonwealth to consider assuming responsibility for the Territory's administration. Similarly, in regard to the matter of whether Asians were necessary for northern development, the NAL took the position that since the Federal Government had already charted a course of exclusivity, it was 'rather late in the day [for the NAL] to express any opinion' – which neatly ensured that the League would not to be seen in opposition to the Commonwealth.[32]

Most NAL members, even if they did not have irrefutable proof, might have suspected that Chinese involvement had been a vital component in the advancement of the Territory, and that the stance taken – or rather, not taken – by the League on this Chinese question was a pusillanimous one. However, whether for this or other reasons, it is a matter of record that two subsequent attempts to obtain a quorum of members at a first annual general meeting failed. A local newspaper commentator suggested:

> [D]ecisions arrived at by a comparatively few of its members might be open to the suspicion of being by no means representative of the real feeling of the great majority of members of the League or of the community generally … In the opinion of many any prospects which might have existed of developing the agricultural resources of the settlement have been hopelessly quashed – for at least many years to come – by recent Federal legislation, and the thousands of pounds which have been expended in demonstrating that many valuable tropical products might be successfully cultivated here may be regarded as so much money thrown into the sea – for it is a foregone conclusion that without the requisite labour these products cannot be profitably grown, and the Federal Parliament, in its wisdom, has decided that in the alleged interests of Australia as a whole this labour must be excluded … There is no use in attempting to disguise the fact that the Territory, through a long course of blundering mismanagement, is at present between 'the devil and the deep blue sea', that heroic measures are needed, and that never was there greater need than now exists for the good offices of a live and determined League in assisting to bring about the inauguration of a bolder and more effective policy, in which lies the only hope of dragging the Territory from the quagmire, in which it is smothering.[33]

In Darwin, the Chinese community had not disappeared in spite of any unpleasantness produced by the racially inspired federal legislation or the lack of support from the local NAL for the Territory's Chinese residents. In September 1906, 'a great fanfare of Chinese gongs and other musical instruments' took place in the Chinese precinct, 'accompanied by crackling outbursts of Chinese fireworks' – possibly as part of the August Moon Festival, although a local newspaper journalist insisted that it was the Chinese community's way of giving thanks for recent rain! In addition, Chinese mining teams, such as the Yap Sue and Ah Tie groups, continued operating in the Territory.[34] Chinese merchants similarly continued managing their business houses, and Cheon and others still cooked.

Cheon sailed for Hong Kong on 26 April 1909 aboard the *Aldenham* for a visit home, returning to Darwin at the end of August 1910 on the *Taiyuan*. Coincidently, Cheon and Joe Bradshaw also shared in common a birth year, 1854, so both were born during the Year of the Tiger. The 'great and good' Joe Bradshaw soldiered on for another six years, until July 1916, when his body finally gave up. The following obituary published by the *Northern Territory Times and Gazette* supplied a detailed summary on Joseph Bradshaw's life and contribution.

> We regret having to record the death at the Darwin Hospital at 3 a.m. on Sunday morning, 23rd inst., of an old NT pioneer in the person of Mr Joseph Bradshaw, of Bradshaw Run, Victoria River, NT. The deceased gentleman's wife and only son reside in Victoria. Paragraphs already in type record the fact of Mr Bradshaw's return from his station per lugger on the 19th inst., and of his having undergone a serious operation at the Darwin Hospital the following morning. We understand he has suffered from diabetes and other troubles for some considerable time past, and from the first the prospect of his recovery from the serious but unavoidable operation performed was not regarded as hopeful. He suffered no pain, and subsequent to the operation saw a few of his friends and conversed rationally and cheerfully. But he looked weak and tired, and lapsing into a state of unconsciousness on Saturday evening, passed away quietly and peacefully early on Sunday morning as stated. On Saturday morning he entrusted some messages and expressed certain wishes to some visiting friends. We believe one of these wishes was that his body should eventually be laid to rest alongside that of his brother, Fred Bradshaw, murdered by blacks some years ago, which lies under a cairn of stones on one of the rugged mountain peaks near Bradshaw's Station, in the Victoria River district. The two brothers spent many years together in that district. The funeral took place at the 2 ½ Mile Cemetery, the cortege leaving the Hospital a little after 4 p.m. The funeral service was read by the Rev. C.H. Massey, Anglican Church. Several old friends assisted in carrying the coffin to the graveside. The coffin bore several wreaths sent by friends, and the inscribed silver plate showed deceased's age to be 62 years.[35]

Among those assembled at the graveside to pay this last tribute of respect were several old Territorians and a few leading government officials. The newspaper continued:

> The deceased gentleman has been interested in pastoral matters in the Territory for many years past; he was a Justice of the Peace, and in many respects he was a rather unique and notable personality – not the kind of man to be lightly passed over in

> a crowd. He was endowed by nature with a splendid physique, and up to within the last year or so hardly knew the meaning of the word sickness. Over 30 years ago, when the country was wild and the blacks a continual source of trouble and danger, Joe Bradshaw and his brother held some country on the Forest River, on the West Australian side of the border, from whence they subsequently migrated to the Victoria River district. There are many worse men in the world than the late 'Captain' Joe Bradshaw. Whilst he had his faults and weaknesses, he was a kindly and courteous gentleman at heart, absolutely 'straight' in all his dealings with his fellow men, so far as this writer knows, and his friends will retain memories of his quips and humours.[36]

Some years before Joe Bradshaw's life came to an end, Cheon had taken up his next cooking position. This time, his work took him to the neighbouring state.

–THREE–

CHEON AT CARLTON HILL STATION WITH THE ALFRED MARTIN FAMILY

c. 1911 – c. 1912

Cheon in Western Australia

Because Cheon had sailed from Darwin in April 1909, bound for Hong Kong, and did not return until August 1910, this would have required Bradshaw's Run to find a replacement cook and gardener, and after such a lengthy absence Cheon would have only held feint hope of resuming his former position at Victoria River. Yet, he found himself a new post relatively close by. Later advice forwarded to Jeannie Gunn informed her that Cheon had accepted a position cooking at Carlton Hill Station, located just across the border in the northern coastal area of Western Australia.[1]

In 1912, Northern Territorian Charles Price Conigrave provided news to Jeannie Gunn of a somewhat bitter-sweet nature. The death of Dave Suttie ('Dan', the head stockman of *We of the Never Never*) came about unexpectedly while he was returning to the Ord River Station where he had been working. He had been travelling in the company of the Hall's Creek mailman. Suttie had bedded down for the night without premonition that he would not wake from his sleep. The local authorities did not pursue an inquest, deciding that there were no suspicious circumstances connected with the death. As a softener to this unhappy news, Price Conigrave wrote in a footnote that he had also met our Cheon at Carlton Hill some time earlier, as he and his party had been passing through the cattle station where Cheon worked. By late February, he mentioned that Cheon was expected to be in Darwin but would soon be returning to Carlton Hill.[2]

James Alfred Martin, originally from South Australia,[3] joined the British company Bovril Australian Estates Ltd as its Carlton Hill overseer in 1909, and he and his family continued in this management role until 1926. Quite possibly, Cheon joined Carlton Hill during the first two years of Alfred Martin's appointment as its manager. Selected as the location, a century later, for 'Far Away Downs' in the film *Australia*, the homestead was situated 'on the banks of a lily-covered billabong'[4] with the cookhouse and storehouse about 100 yards away. Could it have been the confinement of Beatrice Martin in Perth, Western Australia, in 1911, and the impending arrival of their third child that expedited the need for a station cook, bringing Cheon to Carlton Hill? As far as is known, this was the first time that Cheon had cooked for a household with children.

> J.A. Martin trained as a butcher, working in the early days in one of the Western Australian shops of Connor, Doherty and Durack. He was diligent in his work, and conscientious. When the firm quit the butchering business, Martin was offered a job in the Kimberleys, droving. Martin remained on Carlton for seventeen years, a feat of endurance eclipsed only by his nineteen-year tenancy of the Wickham homestead.
>
> Martin (often referred to as 'Hell-fire Alf', because of his habit of driving his car 'flat out' always, irrespective of the state of the road or his passengers' nerves), though not one of the 'great' cattlemen, was an outstanding administrator.

> Furthermore, he knew all there was to be known of the meat industry. He picked the most suitable men to run his stock-camps, and kept employee turnover to a minimum. He was further assisted by one of the ablest bookkeepers in the north.[5]

Although livestock arrived at Carlton Hill Station by being driven overland, people generally travelled first by ship to the port of Wyndham before then covering the final stage of forty miles by land. With the Bradshaw brothers' vessels servicing Wyndham, this arrangement could have provided opportunities for Cheon when travelling to or from Darwin to have occasional contact with his former employer, Joe Bradshaw, or with Bradshaw's Run staff, as well as to gather items of news about Jeannie Gunn from time to time.

Carlton Hill Station's lease was first taken up in 1883 by the Durack brothers, but the holding was transferred to the Hart brothers about a year later. In 1897, the station lease was transferred to another Hart brother, Herbert, who previously had been working at Victoria River Downs Station.

> Herbert Hart placed his little camp next to a natural spring and with a few horses, and old dray, a cook and several Aboriginal stockmen, started to build the station. He had purchased some cattle from Victoria River Downs and he walked them across after the Wet of 1898 to start his Carlton Hill herd ... After five years without leaving the station, he sold the lease to S.R. and I.S. Emanuel who in 1907 transferred to Emanuel, Kidman and Troup. Bovril Australian Estates took over in 1909.[6]

During the years when Cheon cooked at Carlton Hill Station, Wyndham might be sensibly described as a relatively unpretentious settlement. Florence Martin, who was born at Wyndham in 1909, described the port as being 'just a single strip of street between the muddy waters of Cambridge Gulf and the high range of The Bastion and Mount Albany. Along either side of the street, lined with Boab trees, was a sprinkling of corrugated iron-roofed houses and a few shops owned by both Chinese and Whites.'[7] In the street there also stood the two-storey Wyndham Hotel, which had been built in 1897.[8] 'Opposite the hotel was the goods shed and at the back of this a jetty ran out into the muddy waters of the gulf.'[9]

In Martin family history, the name of Cheon, the cook, appeared on three separate occasions. The first of these was the heartbreaking burial of the young Ethel Martin, who died in 1923 while still a child. Ethel's older sister Florence recalled that as her father read the burial service, the others in attendance included her mother, other siblings, Percy Pretlove, family friend and former head stockman at Carlton Hill, and Cheon, the Chinese cook.[10] Then on another occasion, Beatrice Martin, the matriarch, recounted that as she and her family left Carlton Hill accompanying her husband to his new position as manager of Victoria River Downs in 1926, the 'tears poured down old cook Cheon's face, [and] the aboriginal women wailed loudly, as our children sobbed their farewells'.[11] And on the third and final occasion, Alfred Martin simply remembered Cheon by saying that he was wonderful and 'and just as good as Mrs Gunn painted him'.[12] Of these three references made by members of the Martin family, only Alfred Martin's Cheon seemed to be verifiable as Cheon of the *Never Never*. In 1919, our Cheon (Hung Bak Cheong) sailed from Darwin and did not return to Australia.

Not all of the Martin stories about Chinese cooks were remembered with the warmth associated with those that mention a cook named Cheon. Florence Martin recounted another family story usually told by her mother, Beatrice. Mrs Martin claimed that when she first came to Carlton Hill, she feared the local Aborigines. Her husband went away from the homestead 'for weeks at a time, out bush branding calves and mustering bullocks', and during these periods, the only man at the station was their Chinese cook.[13] Local events may have contributed to her feelings of anxiety. Only a few years earlier, Jerry Skeahan, manager of the Auvergne Station, located not so far from Carlton Hill, had been killed by the fierce coastal Aborigines during the same massacre which claimed the lives of Fred Bradshaw, Dannock and Egeroffe.[14] The site of Carlton Hill Station was sufficiently near the coast for the threat of attack to carry some weight.

On one occasion when Alfred Martin was again away, 'bush' Aborigines raided the station's storehouse, according to Beatrice Martin. 'The out-buildings of the store, kitchen, and men's quarters combined was a short distance from the house.' The terrified cook retreated to the homestead, where Mrs Martin happened to be at the time. She loaded the gun left by her husband for such emergencies and fired a shot through the open window, not hitting anything or anyone, apparently. 'The cook was no help … as he was even afraid of the weapon. When she shoved the gun into his hands he quickly pushed it back at her.' Although the shot frightened the intruders, they still carried off a cache of stores and a batch of freshly baked bread.[15] Once again, in this story the identity of the anxious Chinese cook was not disclosed. If readers recall our Cheon's hunting prowess with the rifle, and his martial art abilities, it does not seem feasible that his reactions to such a raiding party would have been thus described.

Even before Cheon had taken this position cooking for the Martin family, progress was gradually lumbering towards Carlton Hill and improving the traveller's lot between Carlton Hill and Victoria River Downs. During the same year that Joseph Bradshaw travelled to Melbourne to deliver his talk on the Northern Territory, and Senator Story paid his visit to Victoria River, a new track was opened connecting Brock's Creek with Bradshaw's Run, so reducing the time taken for this overland journey.

> Not the least important factor in the future prosperity of the Depot is the opening of a route from Brock's Creek to Bradshaw's Station (which is about 22 miles across country from the Depot). Travellers returning overland from Palmerston to Wave Hill and the Downs will avoid a very long detour by this short cut and it promises to become very popular.
>
> [Our contributor informs us that the new route from the Depot to Brock's Creek will be only about 140 miles in length, that a track is now being blazed, and there is likely to be steady traffic on it as soon as the wet season is over. – Ed.][16]

After Cheon returned to Carlton Hill in early 1912, he perhaps continued working there for twelve months or more before making another of his customary trips to China, in 1913.[17] It would seem that Cheon's time spent working for the Martin family had been happy. Death did not visit Carlton Hill Station until many years after our Cheon had left, but this, as has already been discussed, had not been the case for Elsey Station or Bradshaw's Run.

Alfred Martin became one of the best known station managers in north Australia,[18] but his expanding reputation came about after Cheon's time at Carlton Hill. From at least one account about his approach to business, it would appear that Martin was little swayed by sentiment or sentimentality.[19] Possibly, this was a 'luxury' in which an employee of an important company could not indulge, whereas a property owner answerable to no one else may have other options. If kindness was sought, the appeal had a greater chance of success if made to his wife, Beatrice.[20]

A visiting journalist, Edgar Laytha, for *Walkabout* (1942), provided a detailed written and photographic essay of Alfred Martin's life as a long-established manager for Bovril.

> Manager, Alfred Martin, who for thirty-two years has been in the service of the English company, deals from the homestead directly with his London chief, Lord Luke … At the beginning of each year Alfred Martin receives his orders – 6,000 bullocks for the Wyndham meatworks, 5,000 for a meatworks in Queensland, orders for Darwin … The manager calls his staff into council – the overseer who is in charge of cattle, camp movements and bullock deliveries, the book-keeper, the head-stockman from the out-camps. Each of the orders is divided into mobs, some bigger, some smaller, and the orders are then allotted to the out-stations … In each of his six provinces King Martin has a governor, called here head-stockman. The head-stockman administers his territory with two white and twelve native stockmen. In addition, two white cooks are at the disposal of the head-stockman and move with him wherever he moves camp.
>
> The herd of the entire cattle kingdom total about 170,000, and is evenly distributed among these six out-stations. On the station are about fifteen hundred horses, which are allotted to the stockmen as required. Every out-station has to muster its herd once a year, has to brand about two to three hundred calves, and is not allowed to lose more than seven and a half per cent of its stock. It rarely does, for a beast never leaves his beat. Even if they roam around in unfenced territories they always return to their beat, that is, to the place where they were born. But should they venture into another out-station, they will be returned by the adjoining man to his neighbour if his own quota is filled.
>
> The manager at the head-station is informed about all movement of stock or camp at the out-stations, the head-stockmen sending their reports to the 'boss' by black messengers. The manager can always check up to fifteen miles where a mustering camp may be at the moment.[21]

Cheon was approximately fifty-eight or fifty-nine years old when he resigned from Carlton Hill Station. While he spent daily time in earshot of the Martin children – George (b. 1908), Jack (b. 1911) and Florence (b. 1909) were the only ones born during his time at Carlton Hill – he had been able to pay much less attention to his own family. Cheon's own twin daughters were probably about ten years old, and his adopted son a little younger. But what became of his eldest daughter, born to his first wife, remains unclear.

– FOUR –

THE GILRUTH REGIME, CHEON AND HIS COOKING RIVALS

c. 1913 – c. 1915

Early in 1914, Cheon reached one of life's milestones: five cycles of the twelve signs of the Chinese zodiac – making him a venerable sixty-year-old. Chinese folk tradition declared the golden day of someone's sixtieth birthday to be worthy of special attention, which prompts speculation about the motive for Cheon's departure for China around 1913. Could it have been a promise of substantial birthday festivities? Indeed now that he was becoming a revered older person, Cheon might have been considering giving up work for a retirement in China, particularly as he had made no effort to secure Australian re-entry papers before departing. Like all Chinese Australians after 1901 and irrespective of their national status, Cheon was required by the Commonwealth to obtain a Certificate of Exemption from the Dictation Test (CEDT) in order to gain re-entry, if planning to return from overseas. A CEDT document usually contained a physical description of the traveller, his or her departure details and two portrait photographs – one of which was in profile. The holder of such a document usually avoided the ignominy of having to submit to a dictation test in English, and then after 1905, any European language determined by the Customs officer on duty.

After engaging with family life for a few months, Cheon decided that he was not yet ready to make permanent this state of affairs, blaming the unpleasantly cold weather of China's south for his change of mind.[1] Thus standing before the Australian Customs officer upon his return to Darwin, Cheon was unable to produce a valid identity certificate in the form of a CEDT.

Could the Customs officer have been concerned that this Chinese passenger was an illegal entrant? Private correspondence had occurred a few years earlier between Atlee Hunt of the Department of External Affairs and Charles Herbert, the Government Resident of the Northern Territory at the time, concerning the 'alleged smuggling of Chinese into the Commonwealth at Port Darwin and other places'. This prospect of Australia's borders being breached caused no alarm for the Government Resident, however, because he knew that the Customs staff at Darwin had demonstrable skill in discerning differences between one Chinese individual and another, particularly between long-standing residents and newcomers. To support his assertion, Herbert described the acumen of a Customs officer who successfully exposed some illegal immigrants:

> [T]o him they seemed not merely to be strangers but to be entirely 'new chums'. I mention this case as an instance of the application of the almost infallible test by which to distinguish between an old Chinese resident and a new arrival – an appearance of freshness & 'new chumism' inseparable from the latter & wanting altogether in the former.
>
> In my opinion it is almost impossible for Chinese coming from outside the Commonwealth to successfully act or even look the part of an old resident. It must be remembered also that here – where there are comparatively, so many Chinese – the European residents get to know them well by sight in the various settlements, and (quite contrary to the opinion I have frequently heard expressed) one Chinese is certainly *not* so like any other as to be indistinguishable to Europeans living here among them.[2]

Indeed, identity complications at the port of entry were something of a recurrent problem for Chinese and other non-European travellers – one not unknown to the influential Chinese merchants of Darwin. Illustrative of this were the difficulties encountered in 1903 by Wo Sang and Hang Cheong, who had been refused permission to land by the Sub-Collector of Customs, W.G. Stretton. A telegram from the Chinese merchants swiftly dispatched to the Secretary of External Affairs of the day at Melbourne saw the matter given some priority and resolved.[3]

Cheon's robust and extrovert personality made it highly improbable that he would be mistaken for an illegal 'new chum'. Nonetheless, his predicament of having no identity papers for the Customs officer to examine remained real. No details have come to light on whether an intervention in aid of Cheon followed quickly, or if it unfolded over several weeks. Regardless, the clock of 'official dithering' ticked on, allowing Cheon ample time to forward a plea to his much-favoured Jeannie Gunn, seeking her help with his problem.

A few years earlier, Adelaide's newspaper, *The Register*, reported that Jeannie Gunn, writer of the *Little Black Princess* and *We of the Never Never*, had arrived in Adelaide on 8 April 1909 with her sister, Mrs Templeton, on board the *Asturias* bound for London.[4] While in Adelaide, Jeannie took the opportunity to meet with Alfred Searcy, a close friend of her late husband.

> During the morning Mrs Gunn visited Adelaide and called on Mr Alfred Searcy, with whom she has been in correspondence for several years without having previously met the author of *In Northern Seas*. Mrs Gunn and Mr Searcy had an interesting chat over Northern Territory affairs and mutual acquaintances in that country. Later in the day Mrs Gunn met Mr Jack McLcod, who was at one time employed on the station of which her husband was manager.[5]

At this stage, Jeannie had been anticipating that her European tour would take at least eighteen months, but in October 1912, *The Register* – on advice from Searcy that Jeannie was directing her energies to a new book about the first ten-acre settlements in Victoria – reported that she was still overseas in Florence, Italy, attempting to finish her new manuscript.[6]

As a consequence of her years away from Australia and her subsequent relocation to her sister's residence at East Melbourne upon her return, Jeannie Gunn might well have been preoccupied with adjusting to life back in Victoria[7] when Cheon's appeal eventually came to her attention. Nonetheless, once informed about his predicament, she petitioned the Administrator on his behalf, only to learn that her friend had not only regained entry to the Territory already, but was also employed cooking for Government House![8]

Jeannie Gunn's published reminiscence of her Top End experience coupled with Alfred Searcy's *In Northern Seas* (1905) had been well received by the public, and became easily accessible sources of background information on the Territory for government officials or other parties. So, after being suitably briefed about the problem of this long-term Chinese resident wishing to re-enter Australia without documents, the Administrator or the Customs officer would have recognised without too much effort that it was Cheon of the *Never Never* who was knocking at Australia's front door. Just how much Cheon's celebrity was a factor in determining the outcome cannot be established clearly, but those in authority unquestionably showed an interest in his problem and in resolving it. The excerpt from a 'Girl's Impression of Darwin', syndicated from the Sydney *Sun* by the *Northern Territory Times and Gazette* on 24 May 1919, showed that Cheon, the celebrity, certainly had his followers.[9]

His Excellency, Dr Gilruth

On 17 April 1912, Dr John Anderson Gilruth, accompanied by his wife and family, disembarked from the SS *Mataram* at Darwin to take up his position as the first Administrator of the Northern Territory.[10] This Scottish veterinary scientist had agreed in February 1912 to accept the post of Administrator offered by the Commonwealth of Australia after it had become responsible for the Territory. Dr Gilruth timed his arrival for two months later in order to coincide with the end of the tropical wet season.

Several analyses of the Gilruth regime, including a Royal Commission, have been conducted and published for an audience particularly anxious to access such material. The information on Dr Gilruth and his administration provided in this chapter serves mainly to provide a framework for our hero's story and not so much as a potted history of the Gilruth years.

As the first Administrator, Dr Gilruth proved to be a controversial figure, creating divisions in community opinion about the merit of his contribution. H.I. Jensen – who was not an easygoing character himself, it seems[11] – had to work closely with the Administrator as Director of Mines and was one of his senior advisors, but he became increasingly disenchanted with the Administrator's style of leadership.

Jensen was not alone in his dissatisfaction, as others were also prepared to give voice to their grievances. Specially convened 'indignation meetings' among Territory residents demonstrated the high level of community frustration.[12] The highly organised Australian Workers Union came out swinging, accusing the Gilruth regime of maladministration.[13] Jensen, in an article entitled 'The Darwin Rebellion' (1966), summed up Gilruth's rise and fall, with an economy of words:

> On his arrival in Darwin Dr Gilruth was received with the greatest enthusiasm and was welcomed by all sections of the people as the harbinger of a new progressive era. It was not long before his tyrannical disposition made him the most unpopular man in the Territory.[14]

Yet Jessie Lichfield, long-time Territory resident and family matriarch, held a more favourable opinion about Dr Gilruth and apportioned blame on the administration staff for problems or mistakes in the management of the Territory. During the early, more amicable years of the Gilruth administration, Mrs Litchfield had been told of a small group of local folk sailing the Daly River – comprised of two men, three women and three children – who were sharing a vessel with the Administrator and his entourage. One of the Administrator's staff descended to the lower deck, officiously instructing those whom he found there to stay below since the upper deck had been reserved for the official party, and that the children should remain quiet so as not to disturb the Administrator. However, Dr Gilruth soon appeared and, after acquainting himself with the circumstances of these ordinary passengers, invited them to join him on the upper deck where the facilities would offer greater comfort and more safety for the children to move about. It was also claimed that the Administrator assisted these passengers when they were ready to disembark at the mouth of the river.[15]

Dr Gilruth may have too readily disregarded the opinions of his advisors, and he might also have been elitist, arrogant and much disliked. Yet, Judge Bevan, in his address at a Northern Territory Civil Service Association dinner to welcome the visiting officers from the HMAS *Sydney* and accompanying submarines, presented a view of the Administrator that was contrary to the one held by his critics, saying that Dr Gilruth was 'a man of strong character, a man whose word must carry weight, and a man who [was] willing to take what advice those who are around can offer him'.[16] Obviously, Judge Bevan enjoyed an amicable relationship with the Administrator – a state of affairs not so easily achieved by others. Many Darwin residents formed negative opinions about the key officials closest to the Administrator, in particular Henry E. Carey, initially his private secretary and later the incumbent for several influential positions, as well as R.J. Evans, Government Accountant and the former Superintendent of Railways, and Judge Bevan from the Supreme Court.

The initially warm response to Dr Gilruth may have resulted from one of his earliest acts as Administrator. In hosting a garden party at Government House within a few days after their arrival, Dr Gilruth and his wife gathered together Territorians from diverse backgrounds for the function. Invitations were extended so that the people of Darwin might meet the Hon. Josiah Thomas, the Minister for External Affairs, and other members of a visiting parliamentary delegation. Besides the many Territorians, including several Chinese Territorians, the guests included such notables as 'the Director of Lands Mr George Ryland, the Director of Agriculture Mr W.H. Clarke, and the Reverend John Flynn of the Australian Inland Mission'.[17]

The newspaper reported on the mixture of old and new Territorians comprising the guests, but the Gilruth photographic collection illustrates just how audacious the guest list was in reality. Greatly enamoured, the *Northern Territory Times and Gazette* applauded the social change being introduced by the new man at the top.

> Three hundred and seventy[-]three guests were invited, and Government House and grounds were the scene of an animated and most sociable gathering. It required but little imagination to feel, in surveying the scene, that we are living

> in days when history is being made and a new epoch inaugurated. 'The old order changeth yielding place to new.' Even the change from the familiar but non-committal 'Residency' to 'Government House' is significant. It reminded us that henceforth the government of the Territory is to be from within the Territory, and that the interests of the people and of the country are to be considered and dealt with on the spot. It is interesting, too, to note the blending of the old and new among the residents present … It was pleasing, and we hope prophetic, to witness the cordial mingling of the 'old' and the 'new'. This is as it should be. Many unwise words have been spoken lately, and bitter words have been spoken in response. The sooner both are forgotten the better. Much has been done in the last few days, to help us forget. 'The Pioneers' was one of the most heartily received toasts at the workers' social on Monday night; on Tuesday night nearly every speaker paid his tribute to those who have held the fort, and the Garden Party on Monday afternoon did much to create a spirit of cordial comradeship. For that the community owes its gratitude to those whose thoughtfulness provided the occasion. When we consider, in addition, how short a time His Excellency and Mrs Gilruth had been with us, and the liberal scale on which the arrangements had been made, the greater credit is due to them for the complete success and the good effects of their first Garden Party in Darwin.[18]

Regardless of any personal opinion held by Dr Gilruth or his wife on the proper racial hierarchy,[19] ethnically diverse social events occurred more than a few times during this first administration. On the anniversaries of Empire Day for 1913, 1914 and 1915, Dr and Mrs Gilruth hosted celebrations in the Government House grounds for all the children of Darwin, among whom may have been Selina Hang Gong and Chin Mook Sang.[20]

Described as a 'happy little function' by a local journalist, the Administrator's Empire Day celebration for 1913 took place on the tennis court situated on the eastern side of Government House. Initially, the event had been scheduled for Saturday but due to the unexpected death of the director of the Experimental Botanical Gardens, Nicholas Holtze, the decision was taken to postpone the Empire Day celebration for a few days. Mr Holtze, former Government Secretary and sometime Acting Government Resident, had been summarily dismissed by Dr Gilruth in

1912 and replaced by the latter's own personal secretary, Henry E. Carey. Mr Holtze died from stomach ulcers on 24 May 1913.[21]

At the rescheduled event, about eighty of Darwin's school children were entertained by Mr Lewis of the Agricultural Department as master of ceremonies. Afternoon tea was served on the tennis court and the drawing room had been requisitioned for a cinematographic show. For sports, the children participated in pillow fights, cockfighting, blindfold boxing, egg and spoon races, thread the needle for both boys and girls, and several other physically active games.[22]

The success of this celebration encouraged the administration to repeat the event the following year. The Empire Day celebrations for 1914 included a visit by Dr Gilruth to the local school to deliver a short speech to the children who, in turn, provided the entertainment for the assembled townsfolk during the afternoon. Children from both the state school and the Catholic convent school descended on Government House where they were rewarded with a banquet of cakes and soft drinks and the almost customary cinematographic screening. The adults in attendance included the Administrator, Dr Mervyn Holmes (Government Medical Officer), Messers Carey, Lewis, McEachran, Congrieve and Andrews, Mr Lampe (state school teacher), Fr Gsell (convent school) and many other locals.[23]

The celebration for Empire Day 1915 was again hosted by Dr Gilruth but this was the final time under his administration that it was held at Government House. The Administrator and Mrs Gilruth jointly presided over this happy gathering. The local newspaper reporting on the children's sporting activities mentioned that on this occasion, the bun-eating competition had been won by 'a young Chinese boy, with infinite patience'.[24]

Was Cheon among the staff responsible for preparing the 'splendid afternoon tea' provided for the local children attending the Empire Day celebration in 1913? He certainly had the credentials, having been able to produce light sponge cakes, scones, fruit mince pies and other sweet delicacies at the Elsey. Was it possible that he was still on staff for the 1915 celebrations? Of the others cooking in the Government House kitchen, possibly in concert with Cheon, a couple were likely candidates for the hypothetical title of Australia's first Chinese celebrity cook.

Imagined contenders for the title of Australia's first Chinese celebrity cook

During the several decades that Cheon worked in the Northern Territory as a cook, many other Chinese performed the same kind of work and as such were potential nominees for the title of first celebrity Chinese cook in Australia. In the Territory, for example, Chinese worked as cooks along the construction route of the Overland Telegraph, at the mining camps, at hotels, on the stations, in ships galleys as well as in private households.

Where Chinese were welcome to apply, Chinese cook often followed Chinese cook, at least at some point in the history of the post. For example, at Bradshaw's Run before Cheon took the position, Williams had been appointed as cook, but prior to him, Ah Wah, followed by Ah Tong (before he was dismissed), performed the role along with that of gardener. At the Elsey Station, Cheon and Sam Lee had been preceded by another Chinese cook. In 1897, according to an item in the *Northern Territory Times and Gazette*, Ah Poy had been the station cook, and John McLennan ('Sanguine Scot' of *We of the Never Never*) the manager. During an attack by local Aborigines, Charlie and Joe, while the manager and others were away from the homestead, Ah Poy was speared twice – once through the back and once through the lower part of his leg.[25] Even newspaper accounts like this in which the identity of the cook was part of the report provide, at best, a piecemeal or anecdotal account of Chinese cooks in the Northern Territory – or, for that matter, in Australia generally. Other news items merely exploited the nameless, stereotypical 'Chinese cook', with an emphasis on sensation, crime or misadventure.

During the First World War, the War Precautions Aliens Registrations Regulations (1916) fashioned a data collection system for certain classes of people. From 1916 to 1920, Australia made it mandatory for all enemy aliens and enemy naturalised subjects to register with the authorities. In the Northern Territory, for unspecified reasons, registration extended far beyond the citizens of those nations with which Australia was at war. Non-white aliens, enemy as well as ally, were required to register – a measure which resulted in a momentum that caught even those non-white Australians who were British subjects by birth. Clearly, racialist thinking influenced the implementation of this regulation, yet the Northern Territory information collected has provided a valuable archival record of Chinese who worked as cooks during that specific period. During the four years that the War Precautions registration was active, sixty Chinese including Cheon were recorded as cooks in the Territory. Some were also reported in the newspapers. Yet newspaper research has identified none in the Territory – or in other parts of Australia, for that matter – who could justifiably lay claim to a celebrity equal to or greater than that attributed to Cheon. Notwithstanding this, there were two other Chinese cooks from the Territory whose professional standing allowed them a moment in the culinary spotlight. These two potential challengers, former Government House chefs, were named Ah Chou and Chin Wah Shoue.

Challenger one: Ah Chou

When the Gilruth family travelled to Darwin, they brought with them a friend, Miss Elsie Masson of Melbourne, to be a governess for their two older children. Elsie Masson performed these duties for eighteen months was well as touring further afield with Dr Gilruth. She worked at Government House at the same time as the cook Ah Chou, the table servant Ah Bong, the dhobie Ah How and the house servant Ah Sing.[26]

Elsie Masson's Northern Territory experiences provided her with the material for a few newspaper or magazine articles as well as a book. In her writing, she acknowledged that the Government House cook was excellent, but neglected to provide his name. Yet, from other sources it has been possible to deduce that Ah Chou was the cook there from the time that the Gilruths first occupied the residence in 1912. Masson described the cook, and the Gilruth photographic collection has supplied an image of him.

> Cook is stout, beetle-browed, and deep-voiced, always jovial and imperturbable in any circumstances, and an excellent chef. Through the kitchen window his black head can be seen bending over his saucepans, or his burly form, in white singlet, wide black trousers, and blue cummerbund, moving from oven to dresser with incredible swiftness. At the same time he pours out a flood of Chinese … His conversation is generally addressed to Chin Sing, the laundryman … Chin Sing is lean, brown, and withered, like an old pea-nut. He looks like he might at any moment slip through a crack in the verandah, and he frequently seats himself comfortably on a jam tin to have a talk with cook.[27]

Despite Ah Chou's culinary skills, neither Masson's writing style nor her attitudes to non-European Territorians provided this excellent cook with the sort of endorsement that Cheon received in *We of the Never Never*. However, there was one other serious contender for our hypothetical title.

Challenger two: Chin Wah Shoue

The Australia Café, once a prestigious eating establishment, opened for business in early 1917 in Cavenagh Street, Darwin. It was located two doors along from the well-known Chinese firm of Yet Loong & Sons. Unlike the two-storey building housing Yet Loong & Sons, the Australia Café occupied a modest, single-storey shopfront. Promoting good cooking as its main virtue, the café offered a most accommodating service seemingly unconstrained by conventional trading hours. Clientele could consult on their culinary needs, request a delivery of hot meals or order picnic hampers, train luncheons, suppers or afternoon refreshments. The café also catered for banquets, dances, socials and formal dinners. Its chef and part-owner was Chin Wah Shoue. Chin had been the head chef at Darwin's Government House for the four years between 1913 and 1917, and before that had been the head chef at the Hotel Victoria for many years.

While at Government House, Cheon and Chin perhaps shared a kitchen either as colleagues or as unequal rivals. Their inequality was structural as well as a matter of circumstance – Chin, as head chef, was in charge of the kitchen, meaning that Cheon was likely a sous chef. On the other hand, Cheon was senior to Chin by age, customarily deserving respect, and, of course, Cheon's fame – contingent on the success of *Never Never* – probably went national once copies of the book had reached Australia, whereas Chin's celebrity was largely confined to the Territory.

In October 1915, the Federal Government took control of all Northern Territory hotels, north of the 15th parallel. In Darwin, this action coupled with an escalating dislike of the Administrator to stir up the community. With the government in charge, hotel standards plummeted, closely followed by staff morale. Publicans were accused of watering down the beer with bar slops. Hotel guests were reported as preferring 'to eat at restaurants rather than in hotel dining rooms. The Terminus was condemned as uninhabitable and commercial travellers complained that Darwin's hotels were the worst in the Australian bush.'[28] Doubtless,

Darwin's entrepreneurs assessed the new business opportunities generated by these events. Chin and a business partner, Jack Lee Hang Gong, decided to open a café. Jack Hang Gong was a brother to Selina Hassan,[29] and the son of policeman Arthur Lee Hang Gong, and grandson of Lee Hang Gong and Sarah Bowman who had moved with their family to Darwin c. 1876 from Creswick in Victoria.[30]

Reporting on functions held at Chinese-run cafés was an uncommon activity for the *Northern Territory Times and Gazette*. However, two particular events wed the culinary finesse of the Australia Café to the strategies of the anti-Gilruth campaigners. Reporting on two dinner parties provided local journalists with opportunities to pass comment on the dismal state of affairs at the government-run hotels.

In these reports, the quality of the fare served by the café receives only brief mention. Despite this, the Australia Café's chef acquitted himself admirably, serving 'a sumptuous repast' on one occasion[31] and, on the other, a dinner 'such as the boarders at State Hotels don't even see at Christmas time, except in their dreams'.[32] It would seem that the Australia Café's fare was close to, if not the best fare in town, but the reporting makes no attempt to stimulate the reader's culinary interests with a detailed description of the cuisine or its flavours.

Had misfortune not befallen chef Chin, and subsequently the Australia Café, his reputation as a cook might have expanded well beyond the borders of the Territory and encroached on Cheon's fame. His potential, however, was cut short when Chin suffered a fatal wound while watching a film screened at the local cinema.

On the corner of Cavenagh and Bennett streets, next door to Yet Loong & Sons, stood the open-air entertainment centre, known as the Don Pictures at the Stadium. There may have been a three-way proprietorship of this entertainment venue, comprised of Messrs Wedd and Ali Hassan, with Felix Ernest Holmes as a silent partner. Ali Hassan became the husband of Selina Hang Gong. Don Stadium was well patronised by the people of Darwin for its entertainments of silent films and sporting events. Boxing proved to be highly popular when films were not on the bill.

Darwin was the last capital city in Australia to be connected to electric power. This modernisation did not occur until 1923. However, well before the town's electrification, Felix Holmes's financial backing of the Don

Pictures led to the venue's becoming one of the best lit sites at Darwin. When improvements were activated in 1916, the light show at Don Pictures added a new brightness and even glamour to Darwin by night.

> Lights have been installed all round the Stadium, on the outside as well as inside; and on the Bennett street front powerful lamps throw a flood of light which renders the whole of that street as far as the Esplanade almost as light as day. Overhead, on this front, the title, 'Don Pictures' is flashed momentarily, in large and brilliant lettering formed of minute glass bulb lights of varied colors – reminiscent of the flash light announcements around Circular Quay, Sydney.[33]

As might be anticipated during a screening, the light installations were switched off in order to cast the interior into shadow. Thus it was that in the shadows of the Stadium on Wednesday 30 April 1919, a shot was fired and a bullet passed right through Chin Wah Shoue's arm, finally lodging in his abdomen. In the local newspaper, the owners of Don Pictures had a notice published on 26 April to inform readers that there would be no further screenings until 'Wednesday 20th instant',[34] but the published date is a typographical error as Wednesday was the 30th of the month. Thus, the shooting drama took place on the night that the cinema reopened for business. After the houselights had been turned on and Chin's injuries were exposed, he was placed in a private vehicle and ferried to the local hospital where he later died.

At the scene of the wounding, a troublesome man named Alexander Schumack was charged by Constable Cheyne and conveyed to gaol. In July 1919 the case was heard before Supreme Court Judge Bevan, with the confusing and contradictory evidence given by witnesses resulting in a verdict of 'not guilty' for the detained man. This verdict was published by a number of other newspapers, but the Australian press apparently had no further interest in who might have fired that fatal shot. Despite lingering mystery about the circumstances of Chin's wounding, as far as can be ascertained, the Darwin police carried out no further investigation into the case either.

No one else was charged with discharging a firearm in a public cinema, and there seemed to be no additional information about a man who had a gun in his hand at the Stadium just before the weapon was taken from him by Harry 'Dopey' Smith. The man with the gun (not Schumack) remained unidentified.

A myriad of questions arise from the details available about chef Chin's death. Here are just a few of them. Was Chin the intended victim of this shooting, and if so, why? If he had been the intended victim, could his rising star have been a cause of envy for someone? If not, was there another intended victim, or was this just a foolhardy, irresponsible act by inebriates?[35] What led Constable Cheyne to suspect Schumack of the shooting? Should Constable Cheyne's behaviour at the crime scene also have been investigated, given that his superiors considered him less than a quality officer?[36]

Chin Wah Shoue had been married to Chun Hee only the year before his death. Together they welcomed the birth of a baby girl, Chin Goot Song. But by 1 May 1919, Chun Hee found herself both widowed and a sole parent. Two days after Chin had lost his fight for life, and without demonstrating much sensitivity towards the bereaved widow, Don Stadium advertised that it would screen a film entitled *The Vital Question*, with a storyline that involved a fatal shooting.

> The star film to be screened at the Don Pictures on Saturday evening is a thrilling photo drama in five splendid acts entitled 'The Vital Question', and featuring Virginia Pearson.
>
> A drink – a gun – a girl – a shot and then cessation of the mighty orgy for a couple of minutes while a body was dragged out of the sand hills for the crows to pick.[37]

Unfortunately for the victim and his family, social and political unrest in Darwin overtook the due process of the law in this matter and their right to justice was compromised. Dissatisfaction with the Northern Territory administration peaked. In December 1918, open conflict had broken out between the people of Darwin and the Administrator. Then in February 1919, the Commonwealth recalled Dr Gilruth for consultation, and eight months later, the people of Darwin decided to request that Judge Bevan, R.J. Evans and H.E. Carey all resign from their government positions and leave town. So it was that on 18 October 1919, Bevan, Evans, Carey and their luggage were placed on board the SS *Bambra* bound for southern ports.[38] With these dramatic events, the Gilruth regime imploded.

Among Darwin's professional chefs, Chin Wah Shoue was a success. He was well known in local circles and had enjoyed a public career spanning more than a decade. Many knew him or referred to him as the 'fat cook'. Because of his stout physique, the appropriateness of the figure's estimated age and the date the photograph, Chin might well have been one of those Chinese guests at the garden party at Government House in 1912.

As for those who could afford to dine out in Darwin, they could have partaken of his cooking either at his own establishment, at the Hotel Victoria or at Government House. Chin Wah Shoue was making his own progress in an open market. Nothing is known of the compatibility or otherwise of Cheon and Chin. However, these two cooks may have shared a kitchen for only a brief period. Chin moved to establish his own business, and Cheon accepted another prestigious cooking position.

– FIVE –

CHEON AND DR LEIGHTON-JONES, CHIEF MEDICAL OFFICER FOR THE NORTHERN TERRITORY

c. 1916

Two strong references link Cheon with Dr Henry Leighton-Jones, in addition to one that is less precise. In the Northern Territory Library's Peter Spillett Collection, one unidentified informant on the Chinese of Darwin claimed that Cheon was cooking for the doctor's household,[1] and the caption for a photograph of Hong Pak Cheong, credited to the photographer W.J. Barnes, provides the second source.[2] The third reference comes from an article published during 1943, in *Walkabout*, which reiterates the comment from a manuscript prepared by John Leighton-Jones (the doctor's son), that an unidentified Chinese cook and an American mechanic-driver comprised the doctor's support team.[3]

From 1 February 1916, Henry Leighton-Jones (1868–1943), formerly of Moss Vale, New South Wales, became a member of the Northern Territory elite with his appointment to the position of Acting Chief Medical Officer.[4] However, travelling to the Territory had not been Leighton-Jones's original plan. In late 1914, his good reputation had suffered a major assault. Dr Leighton-Jones was charged with professional impropriety towards a fourteen-year-old girl who had been under his dental care during October and November at Mittagong. The matter was heard before judge and jury at the Central Criminal Court of New South Wales. The doctor pleaded his innocence and his legal team pointed to his 'excellent public reputation' and extensive community service as the strength of their defence. The jury was not convinced by the prosecution's arguments and the doctor was subsequently acquitted.[5]

Irrespective of the outcome of the case, innuendo and community gossip were perhaps less easy to quell – after all, Leighton-Jones was an unmarried, forty-six-year-old man. So, the doctor decided on a course of action as he faced the uncertain outcome of the impropriety charges. Early in 1915, he made an application to join Australia's war effort. Perhaps he thought that absenting himself from the Moss Vale community for the period of the war might assist with the recovery of some of his social and professional standing damaged by the court case.

In early 1915, Leighton-Jones had put himself forward to join the First World War but his application was declined. Despite being forty-six years old and having had a kidney removed, he seemed not to have expected rejection. The Moss Vale community had given him a citizen's farewell and presented him with a gift of binoculars on 24 February 1915, so knowledge of his application to enlist was widespread, as, too, became his subsequent disappointment.

The Moss Vale doctor headed for the Top End during the second half of 1915. After divesting himself of his medical and dental practice, as well as leasing his freehold property and making his car available for rent,[6] he set off seeking some new, worthwhile endeavour.

Although appointed to a position of importance in the Northern Territory, Leighton-Jones was not born to privilege. His first jobs were in the office of a local colliery and at a country post office, and in order to matriculate, he attended night school.

> Leighton Jones was a well educated and very experienced doctor, dentist and pharmacist – a very self-sufficient man. He is described as a modest man with a great sense of humour; impatient, punctual, and outspoken with a tendency to be a perfectionist; one who had known poverty as a child, mending his own shoes, and made his own toothpaste.[7]

With the asset of his extensive qualifications and matching experiences, including the ups and downs of life, a professional such as Leighton-Jones would have been welcomed by many Australian communities. For the health services in the Northern Territory and its community, Leighton-Jones's relocation to Darwin was a stroke of luck for at least three key reasons.

First, the incumbent Chief Medical Officer, Dr Mervyn Holmes, was intending to enlist to join the war and, as a consequence, the Gilruth administration was about to be faced with the task of filling a significant vacancy while the whole country was preoccupied with the war effort. Dr Leighton-Jones's arrival was timely. On 3 February 1916, Dr Holmes was farewelled by 'a small but cheery gathering' of select men, before the former Chief Medical Officer sailed southward on the SS *Montoro*. Holmes's farewell was an evening of speeches, toasts, music and patriotic songs, shared by the Administrator, the Mayor, Judge Bevan, J.R. Evans and several other public service officers as well as Dr Holmes's recently appointed successor.[8]

Second, Leighton-Jones's approach, perhaps refreshingly, brought authentic authority to the position of Chief Medical Officer. During the year before Leighton-Jones arrived, public disquiet had begun to increase over the conflicted relationship between the Central Health Board and the Local Health Board. The supreme authority in the Central Board of Health was Administrator Gilruth, and as a one-man Central Board 'he ha[d] at times, if not continuously, delegated his powers to Dr Holmes'.[9] Whether the power lay with the Administrator or Chief Medical Officer, the resultant autocratic style became steadily unpopular with many. The local newspaper reported that the Central Board appeared unperturbed about condemning 'hundreds, if not thousands, of pounds worth of property', which, if deemed uninhabitable or razed, the administration would struggle to replace. The Board also stood accused of depopulating the Territory by pushing out the Chinese residents, and by failing to replace them with others.[10]

In early 1915, civic concern led to the convening of a well-attended public meeting. Clearly, the attendees felt that their views as citizens were being undervalued. They aspired to have 'local opinion and experience' better influence the administration of the Territory, and expressed the opinion that the viability of the Gilruth regime would be better assured if it recruited the support of the people.[11]

The new appointee, Leighton-Jones, had a different personality to the departing Chief Medical Officer. Darwin residents warmed to Leighton-Jones not only as an accessible professional but also as a good citizen with a demonstrated commitment to civic responsibility.[12]

The third key reason for the Northern Territory to celebrate Leighton-Jones's appointment was the exceptional expertise and capability that he brought to the job of Chief Medical Officer, as well as to his later simultaneous appointments including those as the Territory's Chief Health Officer, Quarantine Officer and Protector of Aborigines. The former incumbent, Holmes, had been a new graduate in Medicine before his appointment, so he 'did not come to Darwin with any special qualifications or experience as a Health Officer' nor even as a general practitioner. Holmes's tenure as Chief Medical Officer had lasted for sixteen months.[13]

Leighton-Jones's attitude to his responsibilities gained the respect and admiration of the residents of Darwin. Darwin-born Mook Sang Chin, who was thirteen years old during the year when Dr Jones arrived, described him was a 'clever doctor' who always attended when called.[14] At a farewell function in honour of Leighton-Jones and widely supported by Darwin residents, more than one speaker commented on his exemplary civic attitude as well as his dedication as a medical practitioner. In contrast to Holmes's small farewell gathering of 1916, attended exclusively by the upper echelon, the tributes to Leighton-Jones reflected the broad popularity achieved by the former doctor from Moss Vale.

> His services were always at the disposal of everyone, without regard to creed, color or politics. Dr Jones had also proved himself a good citizen, and he had supported every social function either by his presence or a donation of his money.[15]

During 1915, Government House was in the enviable position of having too many good cooks. Before Cheon took the position cooking for the Acting Chief Medical Officer, it would not have been unusual for a visitor such as Leighton-Jones to have dined at Government House, tasting there the culinary skills of either Chin Wah Shoue or Cheon, or of both.

How to maintain a good supply of servants in the Northern Territory – for those who needed such lingering colonial luxury – was deemed highly important and exercised the minds of more than a few. As the newly appointed Acting Medical Officer, who in addition was unmarried, Leighton-Jones would have been expected to use such staff to manage the running of his household and to prepare his meals. With this kind of position in the offering, Cheon, it seems, welcomed the chance to command, once again, his own culinary domain, and to remove himself from under the supervision of the head chef at Government House.

In lieu of any records of the time when Cheon cooked meals for Leighton-Jones, one has to imagine the nature of their relationship. Leighton-Jones – thought capable of showing a great sense of humour, impatience, punctuality, outspokenness and perfectionism – may have perceived his cook, Cheon, during the many months of their association, to be a man of similar qualities and traits as his own. However, whether these apparent similarities between the two led to a mutual bonding or to friction is unknown.

Unfortunately for Cheon, illness overcame him in 1916 or 1917. Although we do not know of his diagnosis, he was so affected that he required hospitalisation for some time, according to a letter written on his behalf, possibly by Felix Ernest Holmes. By November 1917, he had regained his health sufficiently to be cooking again, but by then he had accepted a new position within the Holmes household.[16]

As for Dr Henry Leighton-Jones, the war effort sought to recruit further medically trained professionals and so, in 1917, he was finally able to join 'the Royal Australian Medical Corps as a dentist, with the rank of captain'.[17] In 1923, he pursued a growing interest in tropical medicine,[18] retiring in early 1927 from his Northern Territory government positions and in 1928 from private practice.[19] In his retirement, Leighton-Jones travelled to Paris to study gland-grafting under the Russian-born Professor Serge Voronoff. He intended to learn the Voronoff surgical techniques of transplant operation.[20] Through his own subsequent transplant work, Leighton-Jones may deserve credit for discovery of the Rhesus factor.[21] However, on the very day – 24 October 1943 – he was to deliver a paper on his research and procedures at a New South Wales postgraduate gathering at the Newcastle Hospital, he collapsed and died.[22]

– SIX–

CHEON COOKS FOR ONE OF DARWIN'S MOST COMMERCIALLY POWERFUL MEN

1917–1919

By 1917, Cheon, then aged sixty-three, had joined the household of the exceptionally wealthy entrepreneur and businessman, Felix Ernest Holmes,[1] whose residence was located within the hub of Darwin town. We know this because of a letter written in late 1917 on Cheon's behalf, to his friend Jeannie Gunn.

Like Cheon, Felix Holmes was one of the long-standing residents of the Northern Territory. As each of the two men had an established reputation, it is highly likely that each knew of the other before Cheon came on staff.

Holmes had come to Darwin in 1887 to work for his maternal uncle, William Lawrie.[2]

From a mere Darwin butcher to a beef baron, William Lawrie had secured for himself such a stronghold over the local industry that, when the Bradshaw brothers wanted to sell their cattle in 1905, they knew that the buyer would almost certainly be Lawrie. It was not unknown for him to enter negotiations to buy livestock, then manoeuvre to lower the price by alleging that the bullocks were in poor condition. Albeit in a limited way, his only competition was two Chinese butchers, but once their quotas had been met, Lawrie could once again take command of the field.[3] Towards the end of the nineteenth century, enthusiasm for horse racing and race betting had found a home in the Territory.[4] Lawrie had the financial resources to join the trend, becoming both a horse breeder and a racing enthusiast.[5] However, in January 1913, Lawrie retired from business by selling his butchery and his bakery to his nephew, Felix Holmes.[6]

Through this changing-of-the-guard, Holmes gained a huge business advantage that became the basis for his reputation. As Bev Phelts claims in her definitive study on Felix Holmes and the business association between nephew and uncle, 'Lawrie was regarded as an astute and well respected businessman. Holmes was like a duck to water and was soon following in his uncle's footsteps both in business and his passion for horse racing.'[7]

Now that Holmes had acquired such commercial privilege, he may have decided that it was timely or appropriate to demonstrate some kind of greater civic conscience. Towards the end of June 1913, he decided to stand for the Palmerston District Council and was duly elected in early July, along with Charles Kirkland (editor of the *Northern Territory Times and Gazette*) and Walter Drake.[8] As a councillor, Holmes participated and should have been an asset to the body, but his attendance, alas, was spasmodic. However, the problem was not his alone: council meetings had to be postponed a number of times due to the failure to achieve a quorum.[9] As well, Darwin's ratepayers exhibited remarkable indifference to local issues and a noticeable apathy towards the election of councillors.[10] Despite such failings, one of Holmes's demonstrable strengths as a councillor was his sense of fair play. In response to a proposal to hire out the Town Hall for boxing contests, he moved that the application be granted – even though such an event would have been in direct competition with his own interests at the Don Stadium. The dilemma faced by the councillors in attempting to perform honourably did not go unnoticed by the editor of the local newspaper.[11]

> It is not always the fault of any individual member that he does not make a better showing as a Councillor. As a matter of fact, it is, as a rule, absolutely astounding to what limits an alleged city father will sometimes go to prevent the interests of the ratepayers clashing with his own individual interests, or even his own back yard.[12]

More conflict was brewing on another front. Local control and authority were being tested by the repeated infringements by the Gilruth administration into the generally accepted jurisdiction of the Palmerston District Council.[13] Indignation from the community was not immediately apparent, but it certainly developed over time – possibly with some coaxing from the Australian Workers Union. Amid these escalating tensions over civil management, even though they may or may not have contributed to his decision, Holmes resigned as a councillor after serving for thirteen months.[14]

While undertaking his 'turn' at civic duty, Holmes maintained stewardship over his own business interests. In 1914, he decided to invest in improvements to his business enterprise. He was able to engage for his aerated water factory the services of an engineer named Mr Simmonds, who came with extensive working experience from a Singapore-based aerated water company. This resulted in a major upgrade to his soft drink factory.[15] During the following year, he successfully tendered for a lucrative government contract to supply meat to the state-managed hotels.[16] Had Holmes continued as a member of the District Council as the jurisdictional conflict deepened with the Administrator, one wonders how his tender might have fared regardless of his majority share of the local meat industry. During December 1914, Holmes increased the price of his beef to sixpence a pound regardless of the cut. This business decision affected everyone in the Territory, but after all, it was his to make.[17] However, all was not completely satisfactory. Holmes had to bear the expenditure for establishing an abattoir and a yard, as well as making his meat transport vehicles dust-proof for the sake of public health.[18] Was his product also substandard by carrying tuberculosis?[19]

In 1916, Darwin was finally making progress as an urban environment – at least, the local newspaper reported it to be so. Two new cottages in Mitchell Street, which Holmes had a contractor build, were nearing completion. Enclosed by verandahs and neat lattice screens, these well-constructed buildings of cypress pine stood on concrete posts.[20] Awareness of cypress pine's resistance to termite damage was becoming common knowledge, as some of Australia's earliest cypress pine buildings had already survived for half a century. Around the same time, James Bell, formerly of the Club Hotel and a fellow councillor, erected new premises nearby at the corner of Bennett and Mitchell streets.[21] Bell's building was of two storeys, with a flat roof. Its ground floor, featuring many glass doors opening onto its two street frontages, with overhead fans for cooling, had already been taken by Mr F.G.A. Williams, who intended to open a refreshment room.[22] Councillor Williams opened his new refreshment room about seven weeks later.[23]

The acquisition of numerous Darwin town lots, as well as scores of rural properties, endorsed Holmes as one of Darwin's richest men. His main business holding at the corner of Knuckey and Smith streets covered a large portion of one town block.[24] It comprised his butcher shop, bakery, a refrigeration works for supplying ice to the town, and a soft drink factory with quarters for the cordial-maker.[25]

During what seems to have been a period of great business activity, Bev Phelts reports that:

> Holmes found the time to marry his 'companion'. Holmes at the age of forty-seven married seventeen-year-old Cleopatra Hamuara. Cleopatra was born in Darwin on 22 October 1900 and was named after one of her father's pearling luggers. She was already living with Holmes at the time of the marriage and was four months pregnant. The wedding was held on 29 September 1917 in the private home of E. Williams, Holmes' baker. The marriage was conducted by a Methodist minister and a witness was A. Harum, one of Holmes' butchers. The witnesses must have been sworn to secrecy because the 'scandalous' affair didn't rate a mention in the Darwin newspaper. The discretion would be no surprise considering Cleopatra's Japanese conservative background, the moral views of the day and the fact that baby Lillian Cleo Holmes was born five months later, on 2 March 1918.[26]

Known colloquially as the 'big house', Holmes's residence was located at the corner of Knuckey and Mitchell streets; Government House was its only rival in terms of size. After Holmes and Cleopatra married, the big house became their family home, with its sixteen- to eighteen-foot-wide verandahs on all sides. The lounge room was the verandah at the front of the house, with the ones at each side being used as sleeping quarters. The main house consisted of four rooms connected by a wide, central hallway; each room was large – about sixteen- to eighteen-feet square – but these were mainly used as changing rooms. It has been estimated that the house was about eighty feet wide.[27]

With Cleopatra becoming Mrs Felix Holmes, there was a mistress of the household for the first time, albeit a youthful mistress at seventeen years of age and pregnant. As she probably had much to learn about being the woman of the house, the household was indeed fortunate to have Cheon as its chef and presumably household manager. Holmes seems to have had the good fortune of attracting those with extensive experience into his employ. In keeping the family nourished, ordering supplies and providing a daily household routine, Cheon allowed Cleopatra to concentrate on her approaching motherhood as well as the newly entered marital relationship. Being born a British subject, educated in the Northern Territory and having some background in transposed Japanese culture, Cleopatra's outlook was seemingly international. Perhaps, this exposure to several cultures was a characteristic that she appreciated about our Cheon.

Holmes's kitchen was well stocked with supplies and household equipment. Yet it is not apparent where Cheon slept. Were his living quarters at the big house, or was he housed nearby, with other employees, at a Holmes property a little to the north along Mitchell Street?[28] The cook's room could have been simply furnished with one wire bed, whereas four-poster beds seem to have been favoured by other staff. Despite this, the catalogue of kitchen furniture illustrates the extent of the cook's working domain, and the food supplies suggest the dishes prepared in the Holmes household. In the kitchen of the big house, there were: a Beacon Light no. 8 stove; four kitchen tables – one with shelves; three kitchen cupboards; ample aluminium, enamel and cast-iron saucepans; frying pans; a food mincer; cutlery and sets of crockery; a galvanised dipper; a water barrel; an egg slice; an egg beater; a strainer; a colander; a washing-up table and sink; and a food safe.[29]

In the Holmes household, fresh meat was always procurable from the family butcher shop. However, the food in the pantry contained tinned salmon, tinned milk, baking powder, a large quantity of jam, vinegar, sugar, cereal, Bushell's tea, 'crystallised' orange peel, soup stock, tomato sauce, peanut oil, Holbrook's Worcestershire sauce, tinned preserved fruit, cornflour, vermicelli, custard powder, tinned peas, tinned bamboo shoots, potatoes, dried peas, lima beans, apricots, apples and bottled chutney.[30] From such a list of supplies, possibly the bulk of our Cheon's culinary offerings catered to conventional Anglo-Australian tastes, most likely mirroring the meals enjoyed by those at Elsey Station. Yet, peanut oil is preferred by Chinese as a medium for frying, and bamboo shoots can be a frequent added ingredient in Chinese dishes.

Cheon cooked for Holmes for two or maybe even three years, before he decided to leave the Territory. This step he took in 1919. However, while he was a member of the Holmes household, baby Lillian Cleo Holmes was born. She arrived on 2 March 1918. As baby Lillian's delivery was assisted by the highly respected local midwife, Mrs J.E. Tye,[31] it might be supposed that her mother was confined at home. Although the Holmes household became the third position for Cheon where there was a small child or children (the Martin family and the Gilruth family being the first two), it was the first for which he was on staff and under the same roof, so to speak, at the time of the birth.

How Cheon acted in response to the arrival of this new member of the household warrants speculation, especially if one recalls his enraged reaction on learning that his own wife had given birth to twin girls. It is probably of little surprise to realise that Cheon's outlook towards children may not have been vastly different from conservative Chinese attitudes of the time. The birth of boys, especially first-born sons, was a cause for celebration, whereas the birth of girls generally evoked little enthusiasm. Yet Cheon was not a cold-hearted father; on learning of the arrival of his twins, he mailed his wife a gift of money for the girls.[32]

Customarily, the arrival of Chinese new-borns went unacknowledged until about a month after the birth. This was a social ritual that had developed in response to high infant mortality rates in pre-modern China. If a child survived for a month, its prospects were considered to be good and its parents usually invited relatives and friends to a 'red egg and ginger' celebration. Gifts of money – typically in red envelopes – or of quality jewellery – for baby girls – were given to the child by the guests, and, as a symbol of happiness and the cycle of life, the parents in turn gave each guest a red-dyed egg.[33] Even though Lillian was culturally not Chinese, Cheon might nonetheless have given her a gift of money in a red envelope or jewellery to mark the occasion. Cheon had considered Chinese coins and red papers as suitable gifts for Jeannie Gunn, who likewise was not Chinese. Lillian indeed survived her infancy, although little is known about her subsequently.

From *We of the Never Never*, it is known that Cheon prepared many invalid dishes for Jeannie Gunn when she was recuperating from influenza in 1902, and Cleopatra Holmes (who was almost the same age as Cheon's twin daughters) may have required similar kinds of meals after her baby's arrival. For a postnatal Chinese mother, traditional dishes were usually cooked for the purpose of restoring her to good health, hence Cheon might have been motivated to prepare such special postnatal meals to help the young mother. One such traditional meal involved slow-cooking pig trotters, ginger, sugar and vinegar.

As 1918 was drawing to a close, the Armistice was signed and, to the relief of many Australians, the First World War came to an end. Darwin decided to celebrate the peace by holding a procession and a Children's Sports Day on 16 December 1918. Ali Hassan, part-owner of the Don Stadium, was credited by the *Northern Territory Times and Gazette* with being instrumental in raising the funds for the event, although many others played roles to help the programme succeed. Children from all three schools – state and convent – marched in the procession, with the other significant participants including a substantial contingent of Chinese representing themselves as local residents[34] but also China as one of the Allies.

> A lorry, with the Allied nations' representatives on board, looked perhaps, the prettiest part. Next followed the Japanese with the 'Rising Sun' and other banners; the Greeks, with one in full national regalia, at their head, were well represented. Lastly, the Chinese, who practically had a procession of their own, turned out in great numbers, and their display, was easily the best Chinese turn-out I have seen here. Their dragon, sedan chair, and weird music certainly lent a charm to the

> festival. The chap in the dragon's head, with his dancings and caperings, must have been fairly exhausted when the procession, after marching along the Esplanade into Cavenagh and Bennett Streets, was broken upon the Oval.[35]

Of the Darwin Chinese, just who marched in the procession or stood along the route cheering on the participants is not reported by the newspaper, but as the end of war was a fervent reason for celebration, it is not difficult to imagine Cheon enthusiastically taking part. With these Armistice festivities taking place a little more than a week before Christmas, the likelihood of confluence from one celebratory atmosphere into another was very strong.

Cheon's Christmas 1918 dinner was the last time that he cooked a version of that merry meal for which he had received such accolades in *Never Never*. Although it was immediately post-war, the Holmes household was almost certainly well stocked. Cheon would have been able to prepare all the Christmas fare that his heart desired, making this festive meal a fitting final demonstration of his prodigious culinary skills.

When Cheon left Holmes's employ, it is unknown if Holmes and his family, or any of Cheon's Chinese or other friends farewelled him from the wharf. Nonetheless, one of the images captured by photography enthusiast W.J. Barnes of our Cheon in linen jacket, with umbrella in hand, might have been taken on the day of his departure.

As for Felix Holmes, he secured the contract in 1922 for supplying electric light to replace that already supplied by the government works.[36] His business empire continued to flourish. Cleopatra and Lillian spent some time in Sydney, where Holmes had relatives, and also in Japan, where presumably Cleopatra had relatives.

In the public mind, Holmes led an exalted lifestyle. The circumstances of his life fashioned their own drama. When his health demanded immediate medical advice from specialists in the south, the *Brisbane Courier* reported on 2 July 1929 that a special Qantas flight had been ordered to make a mercy dash to Sydney, maintaining the expectations held of one of Darwin's wealthiest men.

> In response to an urgent request, Pilot Affleck to-day landed in a Qantas aeroplane from Queensland. He will begin the return journey tomorrow, conveying Mr Felix

> Holmes to Sydney for surgical treatment by a specialist. Before the 'plane gets back to Cloncurry she will have travelled 5,000 miles, probably a record journey for a hospital patient. The 'plane is beautifully fitted, and the patient can recline in bed in perfect ease. It is stated locally that the rate charged is 2/- a mile.[37]

The following two obituaries provide brief summaries of Felix Ernest Holmes's life, highlighting a selection of his triumphs from different perspectives, as a race-horse owner, cattle grazier, businessman and provider of electricity to Darwin.

> Mr Felix Holmes, a well-known squatter, who had extensive, commercial interests in the Northern Territory, and was a prominent horse racing enthusiast, died at the home of his sister, Mrs H.H. Mayo, at North Bridge, this afternoon. Mr Holmes became seriously ill at Darwin at the end of June, and, expert medical treatment being necessary, it was decided to bring him to Sydney with all possible haste. An aeroplane was chartered, and he flew to Cloncurry, coming on to Sydney by train in easy stages. On arrival at Sydney on July 9 he proceeded to his sister's home at North Bridge, where he was attended by two nurses. In racing circles Mr Holmes was widely known as 'I. Felix'. His principal galloper, Sion, finished second to Amounis in the last Epsom Handicap, and second to Karuma in the last Doncaster Handicap. The horse is one of the most popular for the forthcoming Epsom Handicap. He leaves a widow and a daughter.[38]

> Mr Ernest Felix Holmes, of Darwin, who recently came to Sydney – a great part of the way by air – to get medical advice, and whose death was announced yesterday, was one of the most prominent men of the Northern Territory.
>
> Mr Holmes was in his 60th year. He was a native of Dungog, and went to the Territory when quite a lad. He there joined his uncle, Mr William Lawrie, one of the leading graziers and retail butchers in Darwin, and later became his partner, taking over sole control, when Mr Lawrie died, of five extensive station properties, including Nutwood Downs, Maryfield, and Humptydoo, besides a number of smaller properties near Darwin. Mr Holmes's business activities, however, soon extended. He became a general merchant, conducted a bakery, and an aerated water factory, and held the Government contract for the electric lighting of Darwin. Mr Holmes leaves a widow and one daughter.[39]

Lastly, this final newspaper report is on Holmes's deceased estate. While some details are not beyond dispute, it reflects the alleged magnanimity of the man.

> Probate has been granted of the New South Wales estate of Mr Ernest Felix Holmes, grazier, of Port Darwin (NT), who died in Sydney on August 1, at the age of 59 years. The testator left an estate here of the net value of £15,597. He appointed the Permanent Trustee Co. of New South Wales and Sydney Seeler Godfrey, of the E., S., and A. Bank of Australia, Ltd., his executors and trustees. Subject to a number of big legacies to relatives and others the testator left the residue of his estate to the Presbyterian Inland Mission for the establishment of bush nursing and hospitals in the Northern Territory.[40]

Cheon was not named as a beneficiary of the estate of the late Felix Ernest Holmes, although there were many others who were. One might imagine that Cheon, now aged sixty-five, was like a grandfatherly cook in the household and possibly had begun to lead life in a more leisurely way by the time that he decided to leave this position.

– SEVEN –

THE REAL CHEON FAREWELLS AUSTRALIA AND RETURNS HOME

1919

Goodbye, Jeannie Gunn

Handing across a silver shilling at the counter of the Darwin Post Office on 21 January 1919, Cheon paid for a telegram of just thirteen words to be sent to his friend, Jeannie Gunn. This having been achieved, he was ready to sail from Darwin. One might imagine him carefully manoeuvring his short, plump frame through the small turnstile near the town centre (that Joe Bradshaw described during his talk to the Royal Geographical Society) and gradually making his way down the 100 steps to the railway wharf, satisfied in the knowledge that he had remembered to do all the important tasks before his departure. At the wharf, steam vapour would have been rising from the single funnel of the SS *Mataram* berthed there, awaiting her passengers and the scheduled time for sailing. Supposedly, the Darwin weather was agreeable[1] as Cheon boarded the Burns Philp & Co steamship bound for the port of Singapore.

Once all the passengers had boarded the vessel, the gangplank was raised and the *Mataram* steamed out of Darwin harbour and into the Timor Sea. By the time the ship was in sight of its first port of call – Dili, in Timor – Cheon's farewell message would have reached the East Melbourne Post Office, for delivery – most probably by bicycle – onto its addressee. This was how Jeannie learned of Cheon's final voyage.

On board the *Mataram*, Cheon was one of nineteen passengers, seven of whom disembarked at Timor. Classified as Malay, there is nothing more known of the Dili-bound passengers except their names. The remaining twelve Darwin passengers, consisting of Cheon and Mah Gin (Chinese), Hara Tohichi and Matasumoro Tsunegoro (Japanese), E.G.B. Dunkerley and his wife, Dulcie Dunkerley, George Lawrence and his wife, Arthur Ezard, R.J. Mallison, R. Jones and A. Way (British), sailed on to Singapore.

Unfortunately, there is also no additional information about Mah Gin or the two Japanese travellers,[2] but of the Europeans, Dunkerley of the Eastern Exchange Telegraph Company and his wife had not been married one year by January 1919[3] and might have been embarking on a deferred honeymoon; George Lawrence, proprietor of Tattersall's Saloon, was a boxing promoter and manager for both European and Aboriginal sportsmen;[4] Arthur Ezard, besides being a building contractor, was a long-standing resident of Darwin,[5] but the references to R.J. Mallison, R. Jones and A. Way are less certain. There was an R. Jones who, as an associate of G. Caird, was in a partnership on a pastoral lease,[6] and there was a musician known as A. Way who was both a singer and a flautist.[7] Although, by and large, Europeans, during this period of Australian history, confined their socialising to the company of other Europeans in an attempt to preserve a certain social hierarchy, the *Mataram* voyage from Darwin to Singapore had the potential to be one of surprising non-conventionality. It was a vessel carrying a complement of ethnically diverse passengers, some with extensive experience of the Territorial life, not the least of them being Cheon, whose garrulous nature would have had him engaged in conversation with whomever. Jeannie Gunn observed that 'in the Territory everyone knows everyone else',[8] which in principle was not such an outlandish piece of hyperbole as the names of persons who appear in one context often turn up in several others. Yet, I wonder if any of these travellers recognised on sight or came to realise that one of their fellow passengers was our celebrity cook, Cheon. Providentially, this small group of people became the last 'Australian' residents to have associated with him in person.

Singapore

Towards the end of January, the *Mataram* sailed into Singapore harbour and found a mooring at the Empire Dock with other recently arrived ships.[9] After her passengers disembarked, the crew of the *Mataram* made preparation for her return voyage to Australia. With her departure scheduled for 3 February 1919, she had a turnaround of only a few days.

How did Cheon complete his journey home? From Singapore onwards, there are, as yet, no details on the next leg of his journey. Moored during the same period as the *Mataram* was the Japanese-registered *Daiya Maru*, sailing to Kobe via Hong Kong on 4 February. Whether Cheon secured passage on board the Japanese ship or on another vessel has to be a matter of conjecture. Nonetheless, he indeed departed from Singapore bound for Hong Kong, and after some time made his way into China.

Cheon's last letter

The last letter from Cheon, written on his behalf by J.E. Tye, was received by Jeannie Gunn in 1922.[10] This letter indicated that he wanted to be remembered to her and that he was now living in China but suffering from increased mobility problems. The letter-writer was, in fact, Mrs Jane Elizabeth Tye – the wife of George Tye, and a daughter of Lee Hang Gong and Sarah Bowman. The Lee Hang Gong family had originally come from Creswick in Victoria to the Northern Territory. J.E. Tye became well known and respected by many Darwin residents as both an interpreter at court[11] and a midwife. In the field of midwifery, as already mentioned, she attended Cleopatra Holmes as she gave birth to baby Lillian.

In *We of the Never Never*, Jeannie Gunn wrote that Cheon had a 'cousin' living in Darwin during 1902.[12] But it remains unknown if this 'cousin's family' was part of the Lee Hang Gong clan or some other Chinese family of Darwin.

Having received Cheon's final letter, Jeannie Gunn did not fully comprehend, I believe, who the scribe was. J.E. Tye has been variously described as a relative of Cheon as well as a male. Ira Nesdale claims that it was Cheon's cousin who forwarded the final correspondence on his behalf.[13] Certainly, Cheon and the Lee Hang Gong family socialised, for we learn from the letter written by J.E. Tye that Cheon had passed many an hour in their company laughing and regaling them with amusing tales of his adventures from the cattle stations where he had been employed, or maybe even from the kitchens of Darwin's upper echelon.

It seems to have been with particular delight and excitement that Jeannie Gunn communicated her news of Cheon to another of her friends, old Territory hand Alfred Searcy, then Clerk of Parliament in South Australia, who in turn forwarded the details onto journalists. *The Argus* published a small article on Cheon the following month. These details have been favoured by a number of commentators searching for details to give a finale to Cheon's life story.

> By the way, I (Jeannie) had a message from the interior of China from my good and faithful Cheon the cook in 'We of the Never Never'. It was sent though a friend in Darwin, who forwarded a translation. Cheon wishes me to know that he would have written himself but he can only write Chinese, and is too far away in China to find anyone to write for him in English. He was getting very feeble and cannot walk far. He wishes his 'missus' the best of health and the enjoyment of great happiness. Cheon is aged about 70 years.[14]

The real Cheon finally identified: 熊百昌

For several decades in Australia, extant documents about Cheon have been publicly available but have attracted little serious attention, even from scholars specialising in the study of literature about the Chinese in Australia. From two different repositories, it was possible to have access to the three Chinese characters for Cheon's complete name, first alluded to in an *Australian Women's Weekly* feature article published in 1939.

> From her father, who was a journalist, Mrs Gunn inherited her love of writing, and her home is filled with books, among which are all first editions of her books, with signatures of all the true-to-life characters.
>
> Even Cheong, who could not write English, carefully signed his name in Chinese characters for her.[15]

We had to wait almost forty years before these Chinese characters were again mentioned. Ira Nesdale, in *The Little Missus: Mrs Aeneas Gunn* (1977), claimed erroneously that an edition of Jeannie Gunn's book with all the signatures of the people on which the characters were based was housed at the State Library of Victoria.[16]

For whatever reason, it is remiss that a photographic image of the three Chinese characters for Cheon's name has never been published – after all, he is one of the major protagonists of *We of the Never Never*. Nowadays, a website image showing the three characters upside down is available. Without identifying these Chinese characters correctly, it would be impossible to trace any of his China connections or possible descendants. Known by non-standardised Cantonese versions as Hong Bak Cheong or Hung Pak Cheong, Cheon's name in Mandarin is Xíong Bǎi Châng. Cheon himself had, most thoughtfully, provided Jeannie Gunn with at least three 'printed' copies of his full name stamped on red paper, symbolising his wish for her good fortune and probably mailed to her for the New Year.

In turn, Jeannie Gunn had been a careful conservator, keeping these items safe for posterity. Two of these are in the possession of the State Library of South Australia and a third is housed at the National Library of Australia, Canberra, but as matters unfolded, none was found in Victoria. In addition, Cheon supplied Jeannie Gunn in 1913 with a forwarding address for Hong Kong: the silk fabric company of Kung Yau Yuen (Gong You Yuan Chou Zhuang), at 249 Queens Road Central, Hong Kong.

From the correspondence exchanged between the two friends, it has become known that the firm of Kung Yau Yuen was still a valid contact address for Cheon during 1916–17. Intriguing possibilities arise through Cheon's connection with this business firm and its method of operation. Developed during the nineteenth and early twentieth century by Hong Kong business leader, Ma Tsui Chiu (Ma Zhuchao), Kung Yau Yuen Co. Ltd became a significant conduit between Chinese overseas and their families at home in China. Born in 1878, Ma Tsui Chiu became known as a senior unofficial Justice of the Peace, chairman of the China Hong Nin Life Insurance Co. Ltd, member of the Hong Nin Savings Bank Ltd as well as the general manager of Kung Yau Yuen. In his later years, he was awarded British Empire Medal and the Queen Elizabeth II Coronation Medal.[17] His origins and the spread of his business network have been described as follows:

> A native of Daishan (Toisan) district (Danggou village within the town of Baisha) in Guangdong province, he [Ma] was known to have business connections with Canton and its neighbouring districts and other Chinese firms in Macao, Southeast Asia, North America near Vancouver, in the case of Canada, or in San Francisco and Sacramento, in the case of the United States. There were, however, some clients who were residents of more remote communities like Calgary in Canada, Clifton, Arizona and Harve, Montana.[18]

The strength of his network depended predominantly on family, clan and district affiliations, especially those linked to the town and surrounding area of Baisha in the district of Taishan, also known as Daishan, Toisan. Baisha, in Area 6 of Taishan, is known to be a one-name town, as the majority of its residents has the surname of Ma. However, besides Baisha town, Baisha district can claim a further forty-seven different villages of which all are Ma surname villages. This appeared not only to have guaranteed effective service, but also trustworthiness in administrating the remittances sent from overseas to the families at home.

> Apart from his extended family members living abroad and inside China, Ma relied heavily and almost exclusively on members of his Baisha group as participants in his network. This means that most of Ma's business clients and associates bear the same surname … Even in exceptional cases in which they didn't bear the same surname they were nevertheless close relatives from either his wife's or his mother's side. In other cases, they were at least from the same native district as Daishan or the same town of Baisha as Ma Zhuchao.[19]

Among the services offered by Ma, the one that was considered to be the most valuable by his clients was his efficient handling of their remittances to China. Almost every one of his network participants often sent money to Ma in Hong Kong. The money would ultimately be remitted to the sender's family in Daishan through Ma's network of business firms and subsidiary firms that were either directly or indirectly under his influence.[20]

According to *We of the Never Never*, Cheon sent a remittance to his wife upon the birth of his twin daughters in 1902, and presumably continued to provide financial support from the Northern Territory between his not infrequent visits to his family. It also seems likely that he was reasonably well known to the firm of Kung Yau Yuen, as a letter sent to him at Hong Kong by Jeannie Gunn in 1916–17 was readdressed to the Northern Territory. At least between the years 1902 and 1919, Cheon may have availed himself of Ma Tsui Chiu's service network.

Some uncertainty exists about the location of Cheon's family. Various remarks imply that the family was residing in Hong Kong, yet other references suggest that his family home was still in China. On one occasion, Jeannie Gunn commented that Cheon had used the English-speaking staff of the Methodist Mission at Hong Kong to write a letter to her. Sadly, that letter seems no longer to exist. The strongest reference to his having connections in China is Cheon's last piece of correspondence, in which he mentioned that he was unable to access locally a person fluent in English. Because he also indicates that his health was failing, perhaps he had sought out family support in China and someone close to care for him.

Because of Ma Tsui Chiu's Ma family contacts, his Baisha town connections and the nature of his network operation, Cheon and his wife may have been linked into this Taishan arrangement. Coincidently, Lee Hang Gong is thought to have come from the district of Sunning (Xinning), now known as Taishan. This adds a little weight to the hypothesis that Cheon and the Lee Hang Gong family could have links reaching back to their respective home village origins.

Should this be so, then the villages in Area 6 of Taishan may have a special interest. Among the forty-nine villages in the Sun On district of Taishan, there is one with villagers who share the same surname as Cheon, and among the twenty-three villages to be found in Tung On or Luen On district, there are nine such villages, six of which are single-surname villages – ones dominated by villagers with the one family name, specifically that of Hung.[21]

No English-language documents record the name of Cheon's first wife, who died giving birth to his first child, or for that matter the name of his second wife, who was the mother of the twins. Even from any other sources, it will most likely be impossible to establish the family name of either of Cheon's spouses. My attempts to elicit help or advice from the Director, Hong Kong branch of International Social Service, with regard to possible Hong Kong records, or from Professor Fok Kai Cheong, who claimed that he had had access to 700 letters which had belonged to Kung Yau Yuen, have proved disappointing. My written requests still await the courtesy of a reply.

It would be wonderful if the assumption that Cheon was originally from Taishan turned out to be true. Then the possibility of discovering more about his family comes closer. Commencing with the surname, Hung, it may be possible to explore whether Cheon's life story and long association with the Northern Territory and Australia still resonates with the inhabitants of certain Taishan villagers.

EPILOGUE

When Cheon exits *We of the Never Never*, he does so with only the most alert readers properly registering that his departure from the story has happened. Unlike his introduction to the story, there is no announcement or expectation of Cheon's leaving when he does. Just before this occurs, we are almost intoxicated by the frenetic activity at the station in preparation for celebrating Christmas. As the station cook, Cheon triumphantly and expertly prepares a magnificent festive meal, the sumptuousness of which could have been the envy of many an Australian home, now as well as then. Presentation as well as its preparation has importance, and having been sanctioned and encouraged to give full expression to his competitive streak, Cheon expends greater and greater amounts of energy in fulfilling his cooking duties, endearing him not only to the Elsey folk but also to the vast readership of *We of the Never Never*. For Cheon, it was imperative that the Elsey Christmas fare outshine any repast that nearby Pine Creek might plate up. Cheon's Christmas preparation was recorded by Jeannie Gunn with these words:

> [W]e assured him collectively and individually, and repeatedly that never had anyone seen anything in Pine Creek so glorious as even the dimmest shadow of this feast; and as we reiterated our assurances, I doubt if any man in the British Empire was prouder or more justified in his pride than our Cheon … Cheon was Cheon, and only Cheon; and there is no word in the English language to define Cheon or the position he filled, simply because there was never another like Cheon.[1]

However, unexpected change was descending fast on the Elsey folk as they basked in the contentment that follows a proper Christmas repletion. Solemnity and grief supplanted brightness, frivolity and hopefulness. In fact, death laid claim to Lee Ken, the Chinese traveller who had barely managed to gain the haven of Elsey Station, as it also did a few weeks later to the popular Aeneas Gunn, boss of the station. Jeannie Gunn, affected deeply by the loss of her husband, soon retreated to the solace of her family in Melbourne.

In writing about this sad episode in *We of the Never Never*, she elected not to dwell over Aeneas Gunn's death but to bring the event to a fairly rapid conclusion. As a consequence of this decision, the previous happy dominance of the character of Cheon, so strongly manifest in the penultimate two chapters, simply dissipates.

In writing the final chapter, Jeannie Gunn, in effect, chooses to make 'no further comment' about the passing of her husband. Her own preference seems to have been to grieve quietly and in private. 'That is all the world need know', she concludes. 'All else lies deep in the silent hearts of the men of the Never-Never … quietly mourning their own loss the while.'[2] The imagery of strong men stoically living through their grief has the stamp of the idealised hero about it. Perhaps because it is romanticised, this summation of the men's reaction to her husband's death seems incomplete, particularly when we count Cheon among their number. By reason of his dynamic personality and garrulousness, it becomes difficult to imagine him responding to the death of his boss by holding his feelings of grief deep in his silent heart.

When it came time for Cheon to leave Darwin on 21 January 1919, in his final exit from Australia, as a passenger on the *Mataram*, the local newspaper, still emerging from under the shadow of war precautions, had not yet reinstated its column on shipping intelligence. As a result, there is no published account of the *Mataram*'s sailing on that day. Cheon's departure from Australia deserved to have been publicly noted, as a Chinese Australian celebrity and because of the many years of inestimable service that he had provided to those for whom he cooked. William J. Barnes, the son-in-law of W.G. Stretton, Sub-Collector of Customs at Port Darwin,[3] considered Cheon worthy of being photographed for posterity and appears to have been concerned to capture his image around to the time of his departure from Darwin. All this having been said, it is doubtful that Cheon's sailing would have gone unheeded by people close to him. One can imagine members of the extended Hang Gong family or members of Felix and Cleopatra Holmes's household coming to the wharf to wish him *bon voyage* and a final goodbye.

At numerous times while carrying out this research, my initial presumptions had to be reappraised. The discovery of a document indicating the year in which Cheon arrived in Australia became a reason for jubilation. This information not only indicated that his involvement with Australia started much earlier than most would have supposed, but also implied that Cheon had worked in California at some time between his early adolescence and early adulthood – suggesting that his exposure to North American culture occurred while he was still an impressionable youth.

The contents of Jeannie Gunn's correspondence combined with a number of other manuscripts helped to identify most, if not all, of Cheon's employers from the time he worked at Elsey Station. With the exception of one reference linked to a photograph of Cheon which suggested that he had worked at Wave Hill Station, research into the available historical sources produced further particulars about all of the other places of employment and about those for whom he cooked. This research into each of his employers and the historical events that befell them provided a context for Cheon's time in their association.

Between 1899 and 1919, it appeared that Cheon changed positions every few years, which seems to have been a pattern for Chinese cooks if not for all those working in this field. Between episodes of cooking, he sometimes visited home to spend time with his own family in China. During the last seventeen years or so of his association with Australia, Cheon held at least six positions.

Contemporary newspapers contain no items of news initiated by Cheon's own behaviour or actions. His name is absent from any reports made by Darwin's police after they had attended crime scenes or raided brothels and gambling houses patronised by the men of Darwin. Furthermore, he seems not to have been registered as a tobacco, hotel or mining licensee. It is especially curious that someone with a personality so large as his did not appear once in local newspaper reports as 'Cheon'.

Cheon ensured that his employers had contented stomachs irrespective of whether or not their temporal fame had already been achieved. Joseph Bradshaw, John Gilruth and Felix Ernest Holmes were employers already in the public gaze when Cheon was preparing their meals, but the star qualities of Jeannie Gunn, Alf Martin and Dr Leighton-Jones were still in the ascendency.

It was not especially surprising to discover that Cheon had already acquired a reputation as a cook before working at the Elsey. In all probability, his competence and outgoing personality made him popular at the settings where he worked and those who came into contact with him remembered his name or spoke positively about him to others.

By making his reputation as a cook or chef, Cheon ensured that there was also strong interest in uncovering recipes of dishes that he cooked.

Through the popularity of *We of the Never Never*, Cheon became the most widely known Chinese cook of nineteenth- and early twentieth-century Australian history, and he was certainly one of the most vividly and extensively described in written form. Jeannie Gunn's writing has been a most valuable foundation for conducting historical research on Cheon. It has also been possible to learn a great deal about the man and his personality though the contents of the book.

In the past, some readers have thought of the book as a novel, and Cheon as a character of fiction; whereas others may have read his name over and over again on its pages but failed to perceive his true importance as a character in the story or as an historical figure. It should be restated that *We of the Never Never* is not a novel. The events and people in the account have been taken from the contents of Jeannie Gunn's collected letters to her family in Melbourne. Cheon, along with every other protagonist in the work, was a real person. Jeannie Gunn employed the stratagem of *noms-de-plume* to protect the privacy of her bush friends as she told of the events which befell them and herself. However, due to a continuing public interest, Australian newspapers revealed the personal histories and the real identities of 'the Fizzer', 'Mine Host', 'Little Johnny' and all the other *Never Never* characters, except Cheon. Thus, the underlying motivation for undertaking the major research project of which this presentation is but a small part was to do the same for Cheon.

Although there are obvious dissimilarities in comparing the work of a Chinese cook preparing a feast of Chinese food and a Chinese cook preparing traditional Christmas fare, there is a unifying element for Chinese cooks of Cheon's calibre. Regardless of the cuisine, Cheon, as the exemplar of all good Chinese cooks, performed his culinary duties with an awareness of the importance of food presentation, attention to detail and professional flair.

NOTES

Introduction

1 See advertisement 'New Fiction', *The Advertiser* (Adelaide), 23 January 1909, p. 13.
2 'Behind the Back of Beyond: Among the Bush Folk', *The Advertiser* (Adelaide), 20 February 1909, p. 15.
3 'Girl's Impression of Darwin', *Northern Territory Times and Gazette*, 24 May 1919, p. 22.
4 'Back to the Days of the Never Never: "Little Missus" Tells How Her Old Friends Have Fared', *Northern Standard*, 10 June 1932, p. 2.
5 'On the Spot: *We of the Never Never*, by A.L. Williams', *The Sydney Morning Herald* (*SMH*), 25 September 1926, p. 11.
6 'An Australian Woman's Book', *SMH*, 3 March 1909, p. 5.
7 *Ibid.*
8 *Ibid.*
9 *Ibid.*
10 'Our Territory', Red Page, *The Bulletin*, 21 January 1909.
11 *Ibid.*
12 H.C. Shea, *Notes on Mrs Gunn's We of the Never Never: Suitable for Both Abridged and Full Editions*, c. 1940s, p. 12.
13 Ouyang Yu, 'Lawson, Gunn and the "White Chinaman": A Look at How Chinese Are Made White in Henry Lawson and Mrs Aeneas Gunn's Writings', *LiNQ*, v. 30, no. 2, October 2003.
14 Lawson's Ah Soon is more likeable, as a Chinese with a 'white heart'. See *Ibid.*, p. 14.
15 *Ibid.*, p. 17.
16 *Ibid.*, p. 10.
17 *Ibid.*, p. 16.
18 *Ibid.*, p. 17.
19 Ira Nesdale, *The Little Missus: Mrs Aeneas Gunn*, 1977, p. 166.
20 H.T. Linklater, *Echoes of the Elsey Saga*, 1980, p. 59.
21 *Ibid.*
22 *Ibid.*
23 Susanna De Vries, 'The Story Behind *We of the Never Never*', in Susanna De Vries, *Great Pioneer Women of the Outback*, 2005, p. 170.
24 Reference to 'Hell-fire' Alf in Jock Makin, *The Big Run: The Story of Victoria Downs Station*, 1999, p. 116.

– ONE – The 'Tiger' Man and the 'Whitest' Man Together

1 War Precautions (Alien Registration) Regulation 1916, Hung Bak Chong, barcode 6561350, NAA, Melbourne.
2 Yow Yit Seng, *Chinese Dimensions: Their Roots, Mindset and Psyche*, 2006, p. 350.
3 Jeannie Gunn, 'Details in Lives of My Bush Folk of *We of the Never Never* until June 24, 1937', p. 4, NLA MS 83, Papers of Aeneas Gunn, 1917–22.
4 William Linklater and Lynda Tapp, *Gather No Moss*, 1968,.
5 'Me live longa California long time', *We of the Never Never* (*WotNN*), 1969, p. 128.
6 'Mongolian Migration', no. 11, *Brisbane Courier*, 30 June 1877, p. 3.
7 Roger Daniels, *Asian America: Chinese and Japanese in the United States since 1850*, 1988, p. 9.
8 Kevin Wong Hoy (ed.), *Rediscovered Past: China in North Queensland*, 2007, p. 10.
9 Elmer Clarence Sandmeyer, *The Anti-Chinese Movement in California*, 1991, p. 14.
10 Daniels, *Asian America*, p. 36.
11 *Ibid.*, p. 30.
12 Sandmeyer, *The Anti-Chinese Movement in California*, p. 48.
13 'Mongolian Migration', *Brisbane Courier*, 30 June 1877, p. 3.
14 Sandmeyer, *The Anti-Chinese Movement in California*, p. 28; Daniels, *Asian America*, p. 24; Judy Yung *et al.*, *Chinese American Voices*, 2006.
15 'Mongolian Migration', *Brisbane Courier*, 30 June 1877, p. 3.
16 From a blue-and-white-covered notebook in the possession of descendants of the Taylor family.
17 H.T. Linklater, *Echoes of the Elsey Saga*, 1980, p. 59; 'Notes by H.T. Linklater', MS 126, Peter Spillett Collection, Northern Territory Library.
18 From a blue-and-white-covered notebook in the possession of descendants of the Taylor family.
19 *WotNN*, p. 116.
20 *Ibid.*
21 Charlie Schultz and Darrell Lewis, *Beyond the Big Run*, 2005, p. 75.
22 'Extracts from Mr Little's Diary', *Northern Territory Times and Gazette* (*NTTG*), Friday 16 March 1900, p. 3.
23 'Country Items: Katherine', *NTTG*, 4 March 1901, p. 3; 'Country Items', *NTTG*, 8 March 1901, p. 3.
24 'Pastoral Notes', *NTTG*, 1 July 1904, p. 2.
25 'Licensing Victuallers' Act 1880 and 1891', *NTTG*, 24 November 1893, p. 2.
26 Linklater and Tapp, *Gather No Moss*, p. 115.
27 *WotNN*, p. 104.
28 Letter to Bob Gunn from Aeneas Gunn, dated 5 & 6 February 1902, NLA MS 9840, folder 2.
29 Tim Willing and Kevin Kenneally (eds), *Under a Regent Moon: A Historical Account of Pioneer Pastoralists Joseph Bradshaw and Aeneas Gunn at Marigui Settlement, Prince Regent River, Kimberley, Western Australia, 1891–1892*, 2002.
30 Pearl Ogden, *Bradshaw via Coolibah: The History of Bradshaw's Run and Coolibah Station*, 1989, p. 1.
31 C.C. Macknight, 'Alfred Searcy (1854–1925)', *Australian Dictionary of Biography*, vol. 11, 1988.
32 Alfred Searcy, *In Australian Tropics*, 1907, p. 339.
33 'Death of Mr Alfred Searcy', *The Register* (Adelaide), 2 October 1925, p. 9.

34 Alfred Searcy, *In Northern Seas: Being Mr Alfred Searcy's Experiences on the North Coast of Australia, as recounted to E. Whitington, reprinted from The Register (South Australia) by Authority of the South Australian Government*, 1905, pp. 13 & 20; Searcy, *In Australian Tropics*, p. 247.
35 Searcy, *In Australian Tropics*, p. 334.
36 Personal comment by Dr Gao Bao Qiang to author; Fang Lo indicated a place of eating, residential facilities and possibly physical pleasure.
37 Searcy, *In Northern Seas*, p. 18.
38 Willing and Kenneally, *Under a Regent Moon*, p. 9.
39 *Prahran Telegraph* (Melbourne), 28 March 1903.
40 *WotNN*, p. 254.
41 Jeannie Gunn's private letters, dated 26 February 1903, Elsey Run, letter no. 37.
42 *WotNN*, p. 105.
43 A story by Jack McLeod as told by his nephew, from *SA Speaks: An Oral History of Life in South Australia before 1930*, Interview no. 8617, Mr Jack McLeod, transcript, p. 6.
44 Jeannie Gunn's private letters, dated 28 January 1903, The Back of the Never Never, letter no. 34.
45 Jeannie Gunn's private letters, dated 5 February 1902, Elsey Cattle Station, letter no. 1.
46 'They of the Never Never: Life Writes the Sequel', *The West Australian*, 11 July 1934, p. 4.
47 Letter to Bob Gunn from Aeneas Gunn, dated 5 & 6 February 1902, NLA MS 9480, folder 1.
48 *WotNN*, p. 108.
49 Jeannie Gunn's private letters, dated 28 January 1903, The Back of the Never Never, letter no. 34.
50 *WotNN*, pp. 125–6.
51 *Ibid.*, p. 110.
52 *Ibid.*, p. 111.
53 *Ibid.*, p. 112.
54 *Ibid.*, p. 149.
55 *Ibid.*, p. 150.
56 Letter to Margaret Bradshaw from Aeneas Gunn (her nephew), dated 26 December 1902, John Bradshaw Collection.
57 *WotNN*, p. 241.
58 *Ibid.*, p. 246.
59 *Ibid.*, p. 237.
60 *Ibid.*, p. 246.
61 *Ibid.*, p. 150.
62 Searcy, *In Northern Seas*, pp. 50–1.
63 *Ibid.*, p. 13.

– TWO – Cheon at Bradshaw's Run, Victoria River

1 Letter from Gunn to Gunn, 18 March 1903, NLA MS 9480.
2 Michael Terry, *Bulldozer: The War Role of the Department of Main Roads, New South Wales*, 1945, pp. 194–5.
3 *We of the Never Never* (*WotNN*), 1969, p. 108.

4 Jeannie Gunn, 'Details in Lives of My Bush Folk of *We of the Never Never*, until June 24, 1937', p. 4, NLA MS 83, Papers of Aeneas Gunn, 1917–22.
5 Letter on Cheon's behalf written by Joseph Bradshaw, undated, Jeannie Gunn's notebook, private collection.
6 Published for the proprietor, J.W. Bradshaw. *The Mischief*, no. 2, a weekly newspaper, published Saturday 5 February 1870.
7 Northern Territory Reserves Board, Alice Springs, copy of log book of Bradshaw's Run, 1894–1901, p. 36b, NTAS 2262, Location 170/1/3.
8 Email communication to author by John Bradshaw, dated 15 September 2012.
9 Port Darwin, 4 June 1905, NLA MS 'Hotel Victoria'.
10 'The Survivor's Story', *The Sydney Morning Herald* (*SMH*), 18 December 1905, p. 7.
11 'News & Notes', *Northern Territory Times and Gazette* (*NTTG*) 24 November 1905, p. 3.
12 William Linklater and Lynda Tapp, *Gather No Moss*, 1968, p. 206.
13 'A Survivor's Story', *SMH*, 18 December 1905, p. 7.
14 Linklater and Tapp, *Gather No Moss*, p. 206.
15 'The Late Massacre', *NTTG*, 9 February 1906, p. 2.
16 *Ibid.*
17 'News & Notes', *NTTG*, 28 September 1906, p. 3.
18 Captain J. Bradshaw, 'Northern Territory Views and Notes', paper read at the Royal Geographical Society Melbourne, 13 May 1907, RHS, MS 000142, Box 49, file (d).
19 Jeannie Gunn's private letters, dated 30 November 1902, letter no. 26.
20 See Linklater and Tapp, *Gather No Moss*.
21 'The Northern Territory: Senator Story Interviewed', *Brisbane Courier*, 18 July 1907, p. 3.
22 Bradshaw, 'Northern Territory Views and Notes'.
23 *Ibid.*, p. 1.
24 *Ibid.*, pp. 2–3.
25 *Ibid.*, pp. 5–7.
26 *Ibid.*, p. 12.
27 'North Australian League', *NTTG*, Friday 10 May 1901, p. 3.
28 *Ibid.*, p. 2.
29 *Ibid.*
30 'A Twig from the Asiatic Problem', *NTTG*, Friday 19 July 1901, p. 2.
31 'North Australian League', *NTTG*, 23 August 1901, p. 2.
32 'North Australian League', *NTTG*, 28 February 1902, p. 2.
33 'North Australian League', *NTTG*, Friday 6 June 1902, p. 2.
34 'News & Notes', *NTTG*, 28 September 1906, p. 3.
35 Obituary for Joseph Bradshaw, *NTTG*, 27 July 1916, p. 17.
36 *Ibid.*

– THREE – Cheon at Carlton Hill Station with the Alfred Martin Family

1 Jeannie Gunn, 'Details in Lives of My Bush Folk of *We of the Never Never* until June 24, 1937', p. 4, NLA MS 83, Papers of Aeneas Gunn, 1917–22.
2 Letter from Mr C. Price Conigrave to Jeannie Gunn, dated 24 February 1912, NLA MS 83/41–5.
3 Florence Martin, *Three Families Outback in Australia's Tropic North*, 2007, p. 9.

4 Susan Bradley, A Concise and Abbreviated History of Carlton Hill Station, East Kimberley, WA, on the Occasion of the Carlton Hill Centenary Concert, 13 July 1993, p. 4.
5 Jock Makin, *The Big Run: The Story of Victoria River Downs Station*, 2002, p. 116.
6 Bradley, A Concise and Abbreviated History of Carlton Hill Station, p. 2.
7 Martin, *Three Families Outback in Australia's Tropic North*, p. 1.
8 *Ibid.*
9 *Ibid.*, p. 2.
10 Martin, *Three Families Outback in Australia's Tropic North*, p. 16.
11 Bradley, A Concise and Abbreviated History of Carlton Hill Station, p. 4.
12 Available at <www.southaustralianhistory.com.au/elseystation.htm> (accessed 12 November 2010).
13 Martin, *Three Families Outback in Australia's Tropic North*, p. 10.
14 'The Survivor's Story', *The Sydney Morning Herald*, 18 December 1905, p. 7.
15 Martin, *Three Families Outback in Australia's Tropic North*, p. 10.
16 'The Victoria River Depot', *Northern Territory Times and Gazette*, 18 January 1907, p. 2.
17 Jeannie Gunn, 'Details in Lives of My Bush Folk of *We of the Never Never* until June 24, 1937', p. 4, NLA MS 83, Papers of Aeneas Gunn, 1917–22.
18 James Alfred Martin, GSNT, Pioneer Register of Northern Territory no. 1751.
19 Charlie Schultz and Darrell Lewis, *Beyond the Big Run*, 2005.
20 *Ibid.*
21 Edgar Laytha, 'Cattle Kingdom', *Walkabout*, vol. 8, no. 5, 1 March 1942, p. 8.

– FOUR – The Gilruth Regime, Cheon and His Cooking Rivals

1 Jeannie Gunn, 'Details in Lives of My Bush Folk of *We of the Never Never* until June 24, 1937', p. 4, NLA MS 83, Papers of Aeneas Gunn, 1917–22.
2 Letter from Charles Herbert, Government Resident, to Atlee Hunt, External Affairs, dated 17 March 1908, NLA MS 52/18/1036–54.
3 'Rejection of Wo Sang and Hang Cheong at Port Darwin, 1903,' NAA, A1, 6548, 245.
4 'Concerning People', *The Register* (Adelaide), 9 April 1909, p. 5.
5 *Ibid.*
6 'Literary Notes', *The Register* (Adelaide), 2 October 1912, p. 4.
7 Mrs Aeneas Gunn, *We of the Never-Never*, with a memoir by Margaret Berry, 1988, p. x.
8 Jeannie Gunn, 'Details in Lives of My Bush Folk of *We of the Never Never* until June 24, 1937', p. 4, NLA, MS 83, Papers of Aeneas Gunn, 1917–22.
9 'Girl's Impression of Darwin' (reproduced from Sydney *Sun*, 6 April 1919), *Northern Territory Times and Gazette* (*NTTG*), 24 May 1919, p. 22.
10 'The Empire's and *Mataram*'s Passengers', *The Advertiser* (Adelaide), 17 April 1912, p. 10.
11 Letter from Atlee Hunt to H.E. Carey, dated 25 September 1916, NLA, MS 52/19, folder 24, Atlee Hunt.
12 'Another Indignation Meeting', *NTTG*, 4 March 1915, pp. 7 & 9.
13 'News & Notes', *NTTG*, 20 July 1916, p. 11.
14 Dr H.I. Jensen, 'The Darwin Rebellion', *Labour History*, no. 11, November 1966, p. 4.
15 Janet Dickinson, *Jessie Litchfield: Grand Old Lady of the Territory*, reprinted 1983, p. 38.
16 'The Naval Dinner', *NTTG*, 14 May 1914, p. 16.
17 Paul A. Rosenzweig, *The House of Seven Gables: A History of Government House, Darwin*, 1996, p. 42.

18 'Garden Party', *NTTG*, 26 April 1912, p. 3.
19 *NTTG*, 30 July 1914, p. 6.
20 NTRS 226, P0001/14, TS 236, Hassan, Selina, c. 1983, Darwin; NTRS 226, P0001/5, TS 92, Chin, Mook Sang, 14 January 1983, Darwin.
21 'Death of Mr N. Holtze', *NTTG*, 29 May 1913, p. 2.
22 'News & Notes', *NTTG*, 29 May 1913, p. 7.
23 'News & Notes', *NTTG*, 28 May 1914, p. 8.
24 'Empire Day', *NTTG*, 27 May 1915, p. 18.
25 'Palmerston Circuit Court', *NTTG*, 10 September 1897, p. 3.
26 Rosenzweig, *The House of Seven Gables*, p. 43.
27 Elsie R. Masson, *An Untamed Territory: The Northern Territory of Australia*, 1915, p. 43.
28 Douglas Lockwood, *The Front Door: Darwin 1869–1969*, 1974, pp. 197–8.
29 NTRS 226, P0001/14, TS 236, Hassan, Selina, c. 1983, Darwin.
30 A connection with the Lee Hang Gong family was another factor that Chin and Cheon had in common. Chin had a business association, and Cheon was apparently friendly with George and Jane Elizabeth Tye, the latter a daughter of Lee Hang Gong.
31 'Appreciation of Mr J.J. Parer', *NTTG*, 3 August 1918, p. 7.
32 'Dinner to Mr George Lawrence', *NTTG*, 24 August 1918, p. 24.
33 'News & Notes', *NTTG*, 31 August 1916, p. 8.
34 Advertisement, *NTTG*, 26 April 1919, p. 11.
35 NTRS 226, P0001/14, TS 236, Hassan, Selina, c. 1983, Darwin.
36 W.R. Wilson, 'A Force Apart? A History of the Northern Territory Police Force 1870–1926', PhD Thesis, 2000, p. 711.
37 'The Don Pictures', *NTTG*, 3 May 1919, p. 9.
38 Lockwood, *The Front Door*, pp. 211–14.

– FIVE – Cheon and Dr Leighton-Jones, Chief Medical Officer for the Northern Territory

1 Letter from S.K. Lo to Peter Spillett, dated 21 June 1978, and notation about Houng Pak Cheoung on a piece of cardboard, NTL, Peter Spillett Collection, file 57.
2 Available online at <http://www.chia.chinesemuseum.com.au/objects/D002979.htm> (accessed 18 December 2010).
3 V.A. Roche, 'Reminiscences of a Darwin Doctor', *Walkabout*, 1 February 1943, p. 27, and John Leighton-Jones, 'A Significant Life: The Life and Times of Dr Henry Leighton-Jones', unpublished manuscript, Mollymook, NSW: 2001, p. 5.
4 'Government Gazette', *Northern Territory Times and Gazette* (*NTTG*), 27 January 1916, p. 10.
5 'Central Criminal Court', *Sydney Morning Herald*, 2 December 1914, p. 8.
6 Leighton-Jones, 'A Significant Life', p. 4.
7 Herbert Copeman, 'Henry Leighton-Jones and His Contribution to Gland-grafting', *Medical Journal of Australia*, 1977, no. 2, p. 870.
8 'Arriving and Departing: A Social Gathering', *NTTG*, 17 February 1916, p. 18.
9 *NTTG*, 22 October 1914, p. 8.
10 *Ibid.*
11 *Ibid.*
12 'Farewell to Dr Jones', *NTTG*, 26 May 1923, p. 4.
13 *NTTG*, 22 October 1914, p. 8.

14 Oral interview with Mook Sang Chin, conducted by Mary Stephenson at Darwin, 14 January 1983, typed transcript, p. 26, NTAS, TS 92.
15 'Farewell to Dr Jones', *NTTG*, 26 May 1923, p. 4.
16 Letter written for Cheon while he was working for by Mr Holmes, NLA MS 83/50, Papers of Aeneas Gunn, 1917–22.
17 Leighton-Jones, 'A Significant Life', p. 5.
18 'Dr Jones Returns', *NTTG*, 16 November 1923, p. 4.
19 Copeman, 'Henry Leighton-Jones and His Contribution to Gland-grafting', p. 868.
20 *Ibid.*, p. 869.
21 *Ibid.*, p. 871.
22 *Ibid.*, p. 870.

– SIX – Cheon Cooks for One of Darwin's Most Commercially Powerful Men

1 Letter written for Cheon while he was working for Mr Holmes, NLA MS 83/50, Papers of Aeneas Gunn, 1917–22.
2 Bev Phelts, *Felix Ernest Holmes, Darwin 1890–1930: Racehorse Owner, Pearler, Agriculturalist, Pastoralist, Butcher, Baker, Icemaker - and the First to Switch On Darwin*, Darwin: NT Research Services, 2011, p. 4.
3 Letter by Fred Bradshaw, dated 11 October 1905, NTL, Bradshaw Family, MS 3/1/22.
4 William Linklater and Lynda Tapp, *Gather No Moss*, 1968, pp. 113–16.
5 Phelts, *Felix Ernest Holmes, Darwin 1890–1930*, p. 4.
6 'Notice', *Northern Territory Times and Gazette* (*NTTG*), 30 January 1913, p. 2.
7 Phelts, *Felix Ernest Holmes, Darwin 1890–1930*, p. 5.
8 *NTTG*, Thursday 10 July 1913, p. 8.
9 *NTTG*, Thursday 18 December 1913, p. 7.
10 *NTTG*, Thursday 2 July 1914, p. 8.
11 *NTTG*, Thursday 28 May 1914, p. 6.
12 'Editorial', *NTTG*, Thursday 16 July 1914, p. 8.
13 *Ibid.*
14 *NTTG*, Thursday 27 August 1914, p. 8.
15 'News & Notes', *NTTG*, 14 May 1914, p. 14.
16 'Tenders in Connection with State Hotels', *NTTG*, 28 October 1915, p. 15.
17 'Price of Beef', *NTTG*, 19 November 1914, p. 8.
18 'Meat Inspection' (reprint from 30 August 1919), *NTTG*, 19 April 1921, p. 2.
19 *Ibid.*
20 'News & Notes', *NTTG*, 1 June 1916, p. 13.
21 'News & Notes', *NTTG*, 20 July 1916, p. 11.
22 'News & Notes', *NTTG*, 1 June 1916, p. 13.
23 'News & Notes', *NTTG*, 20 July 1916, p. 11.
24 Transcript of interviews with Harry Breckenridge relating to daily life in Darwin during 1930s, NTAS, Series NTRS 3205, Location 170/2/1, Breckenridge Harry/Lynch Ann, 1995, p. 7.
25 *Ibid.*, p. 4.
26 Phelts, *Felix Ernest Holmes, Darwin 1890–1930*, p. 21.
27 Transcript of interviews with Harry Breckenridge, p. 6.
28 Phelts, *Felix Ernest Holmes, Darwin 1890–1930*, p. 34.

29 Felix Ernest Holmes, 'Beneficiaries to the Holmes Estate', NTAS, series E103, Box 2, Item 9/30.
30 *Ibid.*
31 The informant registering the birth was J.E. Tye. Telephone comment to the author by the staff of the Births, Deaths and Marriages, Department of Justice, Darwin, 31 October 2011.
32 Jeannie Gunn, 'Details in Lives of My Bush Folk of *We of the Never Never* until June 24, 1937', NLA MS 83, Papers of Aeneas Gunn, 1917–22.
33 Available online at <http://chinesefood.about.com/library/weekly/aa012303a.htm> (accessed 2 November 2011).
34 'Armistice Celebrations', *NTTG*, Saturday 21 December 1918, p. 18.
35 *Ibid.*
36 *NTTG*, 10 October 1922, p. 3.
37 'Medical Aid: Qantas 'Plane's Long Trip', *Brisbane Courier*, 2 July 1929, p. 22.
38 'Mr Felix Holmes: Death in Sydney', *Brisbane Courier*, 2 August 1929, p. 19.
39 'Grazier's Death: Late Mr E.F. Holmes', *The Sydney Morning Herald*, 3 August 1929, p. 20.
40 'Estate of Mr E.F. Holmes: Bequest for Bush Nursing', *Brisbane Courier*, 27 August 1929, p. 14.

– SEVEN – The Real Cheon Farewells Australia and Returns Home

1 Weather described as being 'nice and cool' for a sports' report in 'Football', *Northern Territory Times and Gazette* (*NTTG*), 18 January 1919, p. 17, with no reference to the rain or storms signalled in the report two weeks later, in 'Football', *NTTG*, 1 February 1919, p. 23.
2 See Ah Chong on the passenger list for the *Mataram*, *Passenger Index To and From Darwin, 1901–21.*
3 'Dunkerley–Bell', *NTTG*, 9 March 1918, p. 12.
4 'Boxing Tournament in Aid of the Red Cross', *NTTG*, 27 July 1918, p. 18.
5 'Notice, G.N. 232-14', *NTTG*, 26 November 1914, p. 6, and 'Dope Depot Courtesy', *NTTG*, 16 November 1918, p. 17.
6 'Northern Territory Pastoral Blocks', *NTTG*, 22 December 1899, p. 4.
7 'Red Cross Society's Orchestra Concert', *NTTG*, 9 August 1917, p. 12.
8 *We of the Never Never* (*WotNN*), 1969, p. 13.
9 *Singapore Free Press and Mercantile Advertiser*, 31 January 1919, p. 9.
10 Letter from J.E. Tye to Jeannie Gunn, dated 5 May 1922, NLA MS 83, Papers of Aeneas Gunn, 1917–22.
11 See Ah Jan v. Wong Chong, in 'Local Court', *NTTG*, 9 October 1928, p. 4.
12 *WotNN*, p. 109.
13 Ira Nesdale, *The Little Missus: Mrs Aeneas Gunn*, 1977, p. 151.
14 'Message from Cheon the Cook', *Argus*, 7 June 1922, p. 12.
15 'Nice Girl Jeannie Gunn – OBE', *The Australian Women's Weekly*, 14 January 1939, p. 3.
16 Nesdale, *The Little Missus*, p. 166.
17 Carl Smith Collection, HK PRO, card 34431.
18 S. Sugiyama and Linda Grove (eds), *Commercial Networks in Modern Asia*, 2001, pp. 165–6.
19 *Ibid.*, p. 166.

20 *Ibid.*, p. 167.
21 Dominic Yu Village Database.

Epilogue

1 *We of the Never Never* (*WotNN*), 1969, p. 248.
2 *WotNN*, pp. 255–6.
3 'Young Man's Tragic Death', *The Advertiser* (Adelaide), 14 February 1907.

BIBLIOGRAPHY

Newspaper and other articles without byline

The Advertiser (Adelaide)
'New Fiction' (advertisement), 23 January 1909, p. 13.
'The Empire's and *Mataram*'s Passengers', 17 April 1912, p. 10.
'Young Man's Tragic Death', 14 February 1907.

Argus (Melbourne)
'Message from Cheon the Cook', 7 June 1922, p. 12.

The Australian Women's Weekly
'Nice Girl Jeannie Gunn – OBE', 14 January 1939, p. 3.

Brisbane Courier
'Mongolian Migration', 30 June 1877, p. 3.
'The Northern Territory: Senator Story Interviewed', 18 July 1907, p. 3.
'Medical Aid: Qantas 'Plane's Long Trip', 2 July 1929, p. 22.
'Mr Felix Holmes: Death in Sydney', 2 August 1929, p. 19.
'Estate of Mr E.F. Holmes: Bequest for Bush Nursing', 27 August 1929, p. 14.

The Bulletin
'Our Territory', Red Page, 21 January 1909.

Northern Standard (Darwin)
'Back to the Days of the Never Never: "Little Missus" Tells How Her Old Friends Have Fared', 10 June 1932, p. 2.

Northern Territory Times and Gazette (Darwin)
'Licensing Victuallers' Act 1880 and 1891', 24 November 1893, p. 2.
'Palmerston Circuit Court', 10 September 1897, p. 3.
'Northern Territory Pastoral Blocks', 22 December 1899, p. 4.
'Extracts from Mr Little's Diary', 16 March 1900, p. 3.
'Country Items: Katherine', 4 March 1901, p. 3.
'Country Items', 8 March 1901, p. 3.
'North Australian League', 10 May 1901, p. 3.
'A Twig from the Asiatic Problem', 19 July 1901, p. 2.

'North Australian League', 23 August 1901, p. 2.
'North Australian League', 28 February 1902, p. 2.
'North Australian League', 6 June 1902, p. 2.
'Pastoral Notes', 1 July 1904, p. 2.
'News & Notes', 24 November 1905, p. 3.
'The Late Massacre', 9 February 1906, p. 2.
'News & Notes', 28 September 1906, p. 3.
'The Victoria River Depot', 18 January 1907, p. 2.
'Garden Party', 26 April 1912, p. 3.
'Notice', 30 January 1913, p. 2.
'Death of Mr N. Holtze', 29 May 1913, p. 2.
'News & Notes', 29 May 1913, p. 7.
'News & Notes', 14 May 1914, p. 14.
'The Naval Dinner', 14 May 1914, p. 16.
'News & Notes', 28 May 1914, p. 8.
'Editorial', Thursday 16 July 1914, p. 8.
'Price of Beef', 19 November 1914, p. 8.
'Notice, G.N. 232-14', 26 November 1914, p. 6.
'Another Indignation Meeting', 4 March 1915, pp. 7 & 9.
'Empire Day', 27 May 1915, p. 18.
'Tenders in Connection with State Hotels', 28 October 1915, p. 15.
'Government Gazette', 27 January 1916, p. 10.
'Arriving and Departing: A Social Gathering', 17 February 1916, p. 18.
'News & Notes', 1 June 1916, p. 13.
'News & Notes', 20 July 1916, p. 11.
'News & Notes', 31 August 1916, p. 8.
'Red Cross Society's Orchestra Concert', 9 August 1917, p. 12.
'Dunkerley–Bell', 9 March 1918, p. 12.
'Boxing Tournament in Aid of the Red Cross', 27 July 1918, p. 18.
'Appreciation of Mr J.J. Parer', 3 August 1918, p. 7.
'Dinner to Mr George Lawrence', 24 August 1918, p. 24.
'Dope Depot Courtesy', 16 November 1918, p. 17.
'Armistice Celebrations', Saturday 21 December 1918, p. 18.
'Football', 18 January 1919, p. 17.
'Football', 1 February 1919, p. 23.
'The Don Pictures', 3 May 1919, p. 9.
'Girl's Impression of Darwin' (reproduced from Sydney *Sun*, 6 April 1919), 24 May 1919, p. 22.
'Meat Inspection' (reprint from 30 August 1919), 19 April 1921, p. 2.
'Farewell to Dr Jones', 26 May 1923, p. 4.
'Dr Jones Returns', 16 November 1923, p. 4.
'Local Court', 9 October 1928, p. 4.

Prahran Telegraph (Melbourne)
Vale for Aeneas Gunn, 28 March 1903.

The Register (Adelaide)
'Concerning People', 9 April 1909, p. 5.
'Literary Notes', 2 October 1912, p. 4.
'Death of Mr Alfred Searcy', 2 October 1925, p. 9.

The Sydney Morning Herald
'The Survivor's Story', 18 December 1905, p. 7.
'An Australian Woman's Book', 3 March 1909, p. 5.
'On the Spot: *We of the Never Never*, by A.L. Williams', 25 September 1926, p. 11.
'Grazier's Death: Late Mr E.F. Holmes', 3 August 1929, p. 20.
'Central Criminal Court', 2 December 1914, p. 8.

The West Australian
'They of the Never Never: Life Writes the Sequel', 11 July 1934, p. 4.

Books and articles with byline

Bradley, Susan, *A Concise and Abbreviated History of Carlton Hill Station, WA, on the Occasion of the Carlton Hill Centenary Concert*, 13 July 1993, self-published, 1993 (held at State Library of WA).

Copeman, Herbert, 'Henry Leighton-Jones and His Contribution to Gland-grafting', *Medical Journal of Australia*, 1977, no. 2, p. 870.

Daniels, Roger, *Asian America: Chinese and Japanese in the United States since 1850*, Seattle and London: University of Washington Press, 1988.

De Vries, Susanna, *Great Pioneer Women of the Outback*, Pymble, NSW: HarperCollins, 2005; see chapter 'The Story Behind We of the Never Never'.

Dickinson, Janet, *Jessie Litchfield: Grand Old Lady of the Territory*, Blackwater, Qld: Janet Dickinson publisher, reprinted 1983.

Gunn, Mrs Aeneas, *We of the Never Never*, Richmond, Vic.: Hutchinson Group (Australia), reprinted 1969.

—— *We of the Never Never*, with a memoir by Margaret Berry, Richmond, Vic.: Hutchinson Group (Australia), 1988.

Hauriou, Geneviève, 'Un Auteur Australien: Mrs Gunn', Diplôme d'Etudes Supérieres (thesis), Paris, 1925.

Jensen, Dr H.I., 'The Darwin Rebellion', *Labour History*, no. 11, November 1966.

Laytha, Edgar, 'Cattle Kingdom', *Walkabout*, vol. 8, no. 5, 1 March 1942, p. 8.

Leighton-Jones, John, 'A Significant Life: The Life and Times of Dr Henry Leighton-Jones', unpublished manuscript, Mollymook, NSW: 2001.

Linklater, H.T., *Echoes of the Elsey Saga*, Coogee, NSW: H.T. Linklater, 1980.

Linklater, William and Lynda Tapp, *Gather No Moss*, Melbourne: Macmillan Australia, 1968.

Lockwood, Douglas, *The Front Door: Darwin 1869–1969*, Adelaide: Seal Books, Rigby, 1974.

Macknight, C.C., 'Alfred Searcy (1854–1925)', *Australian Dictionary of Biography*, vol. 11, Carlton, Vic.: Melbourne University Press, 1988.

Makin, Jock, *The Big Run: The Story of Victoria Downs Station*, Marleston, SA: JB Books, 1999.

Martin, Florence, *Three Families Outback in Australia's Tropic North*, 2nd impression, Victoria Park, WA: Hesperian Press, 2007.

Masson, Elsie R., *An Untamed Territory: The Northern Territory of Australia*, London: Macmillan & Co., 1915.

Nesdale, Ira (Iris), *The Little Missus: Mrs Aeneas Gunn*, Blackwood, SA: Lynton Publications, 1977.

Ogden, Pearl, *Bradshaw via Coolibah: The History of Bradshaw's Run and Coolibah Station*, Darwin: Historical Society of the Northern Territory, 1989.

Phelts, Bev, *Felix Ernest Holmes, Darwin 1890–1930: Racehorse Owner, Pearler, Agriculturalist, Pastoralist, Butcher, Baker, Icemaker – and the First to Switch On Darwin*, Darwin: NT Research Services, 2011.

Roche, V.A., 'Reminiscences of a Darwin Doctor', *Walkabout*, 1 February 1943, p. 27.

Rosenzweig, Paul A., *The House of Seven Gables: A History of Government House, Darwin*, Darwin: Historical Society of the Northern Territory, 1996.

Sandmeyer, Elmer Clarence, *The Anti-Chinese Movement in California*, Urbana and Chicago: University of Illinois Press, Illini Books edition, 1991.

Schultz, Charlie and Darrell Lewis, *Beyond the Big Run*, St Lucia, Qld: University of Queensland Press, 2005.

Searcy, Alfred, *In Northern Seas: Being Mr Alfred Searcy's Experiences on the North Coast of Australia, as recounted to E. Whitington, reprinted from The Register (South Australia) by Authority of the South Australian Government*, Adelaide: W.K. Thomas & Co. printers, 1905.

—— *In Australian Tropics*, London: Kegan Paul, Trench, Trübner & Co. Ltd, 1907.

Shea, H.C., *Notes on Mrs Gunn's We of the Never Never: Suitable for Both Abridged and Full Editions*, Brisbane: H.C. Shea publisher, Pacific Notebooks, c. 1940s.

Sugiyama, S. and Linda Grove (eds), *Commercial Networks in Modern Asia*, Richmond, Surrey: Curzon Press, 2001.

Terry, Michael, *Bulldozer: The War Role of the Department of Main Roads, New South Wales*, Sydney: Frank Tolmer publisher, 1945.

Willing, Tim and Kevin Kenneally (eds), *Under a Regent Moon: A Historical Account of Pioneer Pastoralists Joseph Bradshaw and Aeneas Gunn at Marigui Settlement, Prince Regent River, Kimberley, Western Australia, 1891–1892*, Western Australia Department of Conservation and Land Management, 2002.

Wilson, W.R. 'A Force Apart? A History of the Northern Territory Police Force 1870–1926', PhD Thesis, Faculty of Law, Business and Arts, Northern Territory University, Darwin, 2000.

Wong Hoy, Kevin (ed.), *Rediscovered Past: China in North Queensland*, North Melbourne: Chinese Heritage in Northern Australia, 2007.

Yow Yit Seng, *Chinese Dimensions: Their Roots, Mindset and Psyche*, Selangor, Malaysia: Pelanduk Publications, 2006.

Yu, Ouyang, 'Lawson, Gunn and the "White Chinaman": A Look at How Chinese Are Made White in Henry Lawson and Mrs Aeneas Gunn's Writings', *LiNQ*, v. 30, no. 2, October 2003.

Yung, Judy, Gordon H. Chang and Him Mark Lai (eds), *Chinese American Voices*, Berkeley, CA: University of California Press, c. 2006.

ACKNOWLEDGEMENTS

The idea for this book came about when I agreed to substitute for friend, company director and chair of the Queensland China Council Mrs Sim Hayward as the keynote speaker at a 2009 Brisbane Chinese community event about the Chinese contribution to Queensland in the late 19th and early 20th centuries, as a part of the people's celebrations for Queensland's 150th anniversary. While my previous research into Chinese-naturalised British subjects of Queensland became the basis for this address, I thought some discussion on the quality of Chinese-Australian cooking on remote pastoral stations might particularly enhance a section of my presentation. In pursuing this, Mrs Aeneas Gunn's book, *We of the Never Never*, proved to be a valuable source of such detail, especially for northern Australia.

But no presentiment alerted me as to where this offer to be Sim's replacement was going to lead, or that, as a consequence, much of the next few years would pass happily engaged in researching and compiling a history of Hung Bak Cheong (Xíong Băi Chāng), or Cheon of the *Never Never*, as I have come to call him.

The scope of the ensuing research took some novel twists and turns. Making whatever efforts I could to understand the workings of the various Methodist missionary services operating out of Hong Kong during the first two decades of the twentieth century, or the dependability or otherwise of Hong Kong's civil administrative recording system during Japan's wartime occupation, were just two of the unexpected endeavours this study produced. Though well aware that requests for assistance from Chinese family historians seeking to discover the story of their forebears in China can prove to be disappointing, I eventually came to the decision that there was really no other option but to attempt to locate leads to Hung Bak Cheong's Chinese family though such means. The staff of the Guangdong People's Association for Friendship with Foreign Countries, responsible for managing such overseas' pleas, were understanding and considerate, but unsuccessful in advancing my request. In Hong Kong, the staff of the Public Records Office were similarly responsive, providing me with what they could. I am indeed appreciative for all their various efforts.

Pursuing additional study in Hong Kong, China and even California might turn out to be useful and even fruitful, but the trajectory for this effort could amount to several more years' research, not to mention an additional financial outlay. Closer to home, it is with boundless gratitude that I acknowledge the support and assistance, from inception to finalisation, provided to me in Australia.

To continue, the Northern Territory government is deserving of acknowledgement and thanks for awarding this research proposal a 2010 history grant. A number of friends and members of my wider family have generously extended their assistance-in-kind to me: the (late) Patricia Williamson, who without a moment's hesitation mailed on loan her collection of relevant books on Northern Territory personalities; Michael & Wendy Coleman for taking me on a tour of Darwin, Southport and Pine Creek; the (late) Tim & Dawn Forday for introducing me to Darwin's Chung Wah Society members; Beth Rosman for, along with other support, making a copy of a publication of interest whilst on vacation; Liz McDonald for her almost always provocative discussions about Australian literature and publishing; Camilla Myer for generously sharing her practice wisdom; Sue Pechey for her kindly, yet pithy remarks for more than half a lifetime; along with Julia Volkmar, Lorraine Siska, Gao Bao Qiang, Jacques & Margaret Peril, Kim Windsor, the (late) Lola Gleeson, Dawn & Gerard McMahon, Keith Giles & Gary Campbell, my dinner-for-five comrades, and so many, many more, including my immediate family. They all provided counsel, encouragement and good cheer as the months unfurled.

Grateful acknowledgement is also owed to the staff at the National Library of Australia; the National Archives of Australia (Canberra & Melbourne); the State Library of Victoria; the Royal Historical Society;

the State Library of South Australia; the Northern Territory Library; the Northern Territory Archive Service; and the Northern Territory Genealogical Society.

In addition, I wish to thank the extended family of Jeannie Gunn for allowing me access to the Taylor family's collected correspondence; John Bradshaw, an extended family member of Joseph Bradshaw, for so willingly assisting with images and other annotations; and the relatives or descendants of Alfred Searcy, Dr Henry Leighton Jones, and Lee Hang Gong for the comments they were able to provide.

Lastly, my indebtedness and appreciation to Nick Walker of Australian Scholarly Publishing for the positivity of his response when I first pitched the proposal for this book, and to the ASP staff for their editing and support, particularly Diane Carlyle and Terryn Whiteoak.

Kevin Wong Hoy

www.ingramcontent.com/pod-product-compliance
Ingram Content Group Australia Pty Ltd
76 Discovery Rd, Dandenong South VIC 3175, AU
AUHW020912111225
420819AU00002B/27

9 781921 875861